The Beginner's Guide to

WINNING BLACKJACK

by Stanley Roberts

The Beginner's Guide to

WINNING BLACKJACK

by Stanley Roberts

A GAMBLING TIMES BOOK

DISTRIBUTED BY
LYLE STUART
Secaucus, N.J.

The Beginner's Guide to
WINNING BLACKJACK
by Stanley Roberts

Copyright © 1984 by Gambling Times, Incorporated

ISBN: 0-89746-014-6

Distributed by Lyle Stuart, Inc.

Manufactured in the United States of America
Printed and Bound by Kingsport Press
First Printing—January 1984

Editor: *Eleanor M. Saris*
Cover Design and Illustration: *Terry Robinson*

All material presented in this book is offered as information to the reader. No inducement to gamble is intended or implied.

To my wife, Ann...who makes it all worthwhile.

Other *Gambling Times* Books
Available—Current Releases

(See page *231* for details)

Blackjack Books

The GT Guide to Blackjack
by Stanley Roberts and others
Million Dollar Blackjack
by Ken Uston
Winning Blackjack
by Stanley Roberts

Poker Books

According to Doyle
by Doyle Brunson
Caro On Gambling by Mike Caro
Caro's Book of Tells by Mike Caro
The GT Official Rules of Poker
by Mike Caro
Poker For Women by Mike Caro
Poker Without Cards by Mike Caro
Wins, Places and Pros
by Tex Sheahan

Casino Games

The GT Guide to Casino Games
by Len Miller
The GT Guide to Craps
by N.B. Winkless, Jr.

General Interest Books

**According to GT: The Rules of
Gambling Games**
by Stanley Roberts

**The GT Guide to Gaming Around
the World**
**The GT Guide to Systems That
Win, Volumes I and II**
**The GT Guide to Winning
Systems, Volumes I and II**
**GT Presents Winning Systems and
Methods, Volumes I and II**
The Mathematics of Gambling
by Dr. Edward O. Thorp
Odds: Quick and Simple
by Mike Caro
P$yching Out Vegas
by Marvin Karlins, Ph.D.
Winning By Computer
by Dr. Donald Sullivan

Sports Betting Books

**The GT Guide to Basketball
Handicapping** by Barbara Nathan
**The GT Guide to Football
Handicapping** by Bob McCune
**The GT Guide to Greyhound
Racing** by William E. McBride
The GT Guide to Harness Racing
by Igor Kusyshyn, Ph.D.,
Al Stanley and Sam Dragich
The GT Guide to Jai Alai
by William R. Keevers
**The GT Guide to Thoroughbred
Racing** by R.G. Denis

The following *Gambling Times* books
are scheduled for release in September 1984:

Poker Books

Caro's Poker Encyclopedia
by Mike Caro

**Free Money: How to Win in the
Cardrooms of California**
by Michael Wiesenberg

The Railbird by Rex Jones

Tales Out of Tulsa
by Bobby Baldwin

**World Class Poker, Play by
Play** by Mike Caro

General Interest Books

Caro On Computer Gambling
by Mike Caro

The GT Quiz Book
by Mike Caro

How the Superstars Gamble
by Ron Delpit

**How to Win at Gaming
Tournaments** by Haven Earle Haley

**You're Comped: How to Be a
Casino Guest** by Len Miller

Sports Betting Books

**Fast Track to
Harness Racing Profits**
by Mark Cramer

**Fast Track to
Thoroughbred Profits**
by Mark Cramer

Acknowledgements

This book represents the first major revision in a decade of my original work, *How to Win at Weekend Blackjack.* That volume should have credited the assistance of the late Jimmy Termini, a dealer who knew all sides of the cheating issue. While he was alive, Jimmy wished to remain anonymous.

This volume has been aided considerably by several members of the staff of the Stanley Roberts School of Winning Blackjack. These included: Steven Bell, Tedd Hansen, Nancy Shields and Lou Grillo. Their contributions in assembling the field data and designing the study program have made this book even more valuable than the first edition. The first edition sold 20,000 copies at an average price of $23.00.

Table Of Contents

List Of Tables

(Note: Basic Strategy for Single Deck, Double Deck, and four or more decks will be found in the Appendix starting on page 169.)

List Of Charts

List Of Photos

INTRODUCTION

CONGRATULATIONS! You are now one of a limited number of people to possess one of the most practical, easy-to-learn Blackjack systems ever devised. This material could lead to some measure of financial security for you, if you learn and use it properly. As long as the rules of Blackjack are not changed significantly and as long as you follow the directions in these pages step by step, you can be assured of continued and consistent success in most gambling casinos around the world.

Some words of caution at the outset are necessary for those who might mistake the promise that these pages unfold. The amount and frequency of your winnings are dependent upon three factors. The first is the distribution of the laws of probability; the second is your own ability to follow through and utilize this system; and, the third is the size of your own bankroll. Because of these factors, we cannot guarantee how much you will win at any one sitting, or whether you will win at all. That is, if you decide to deviate from this carefully calculated winning strategy, and—more importantly—if you fail to follow the advice presented on how to conduct yourself in the casino, your chances of winning will be greatly reduced.

Since we cannot be responsible for anyone else's diligence or ability, we hereby disclaim any responsibility for losses that both players or casinos may incur due to the information presented in these pages.

This text is divided into four parts for easy explanation and future reference. Part I contains an introduction to Blackjack and the basic rules of the game as it is now played in most casinos. Part II treats Blackjack as a mathematical science, and explains why the game can be beaten statistically and how you can utilize this information to win. Part III deals with the all-important aspect of how to conduct yourself in the casino. Part IV explores the various aspects of multiple-deck play as well as other professional advice to increase the player's winning percentage.

You can be sure of one thing: When the management of the casino where you are playing finds out that you are beating them consistently, they will take countermeasures against you to stop the flow of money from their coffers.

Those who read this book and desire personal instruction and wish to learn an Advanced Level System may do one of the following:

1. Enroll in the Advanced Course at any of the Stanley Roberts Schools of Winning Blackjack across the country, or

2. If a school is not conveniently located near you, we have a fly-out program available. For this program, a specially trained, professional Blackjack player/instructor will come to your home to teach you the course.

Information on any of the above programs may be obtained quickly by calling the central sales office in Las Vegas, Nevada, (702) 731-2867, or our toll free number (800-421-7826) from anywhere else in the continental United States.

You should also subscribe to:

Gambling Times Magazine
1018 North Cole Avenue
Hollywood, CA 90038

Gambling Times Magazine is currently $36.00 a year for twelve issues. Stanley Roberts writes a monthly column in this magazine which will give you updates and inform you on a regular basis.

PART I

HISTORY OF BLACKJACK SYSTEMS
AND
THE RULES OF CASINO BLACKJACK

CHAPTER 1

HISTORY OF BLACKJACK

Every book that is written owes an obligation to its forebears. The knowledge of the world is built upon the fruits and folly of others. Perhaps the greatest tribute to inherited knowledge was paid by Albert Einstein when he remarked, "If my work seems great, it is because I stand on the shoulders of giants." The history of earlier writings on Blackjack follows.

The game of Blackjack is known by various other names. Principal among these are: Twenty-one; Vingt-et-un (French for "twenty-one"); Van-john; and Pontoon. The last two are English and Australian corruptions of the French Vingt-et-un, respectively. The game is played in various parts of the world. Some of these locations are listed below:

1. The entire state of Nevada.

2. Atlantic City, New Jersey.

3. Most Western European countries, especially England, France, Spain, Portugal and West Germany.

4. Monte Carlo.

5. The Far East, The Philippines, Korea, Macao and Malaysia.

6. The Grand Bahamas and other Caribbean resorts, including Puerto Rico, Haiti, Santa Domingo, Martinique, St. Maarten, Antigua.

7. Aruba and Curacao.

8. Various cities in Oregon and North Dakota on a social basis.

9. Central and South America, especially Panama, Honduras,

Columbia, Argentina, Uruguay.

  10. Australia.

  11. Canada (Yukon, Alberta, Calgary).

The present status of Blackjack must be determined by the reader as from time to time Blackjack has been canceled in many of these places.

A complete listing of all the gambling facilities in the world is compiled and published bi-annually by Gambling Times Incorporated, 1018 N. Cole Avenue, Hollywood, CA 90038 in its book *Gaming Around the World*.

According to John Scarne, one of the best known experts on gambling, the earliest records of games similar to Blackjack can be traced to writings printed as early as 1570. The American Hoyle of 1875 makes one of the first references to the name Blackjack. However, prior to the early 1910's, Blackjack was primarily a private game. The earliest use of Blackjack tables in casinos in this country dates back to the horse rooms in and around Evansville, Indiana, circa 1910. Although this implies that Blackjack has been around a long time, it wasn't until recently that much was known about the game. Unlike craps, roulette, slots and the somewhat more complicated keno, the odds in Blackjack are almost incalculable by individual human activity. The number of possible combinations is so great that only a high-speed computer is able to accurately calculate the probabilities that make it possible to discern the proper playing strategy.

The first efforts made in computer calculations for Blackjack were performed in 1954, at the Atomic Energy Commission's laboratory in Los Alamos, New Mexico. The results of that strategy, which actually gave the player a slight disadvantage, were published in 1957 in a book by Baldwin, et al., called, *Playing Blackjack to Win*. Other computer experts and mathematicians worked on this problem of determining the best strategy for the game of Blackjack in the late 50's and early 60's. Work was done by people at Ramo-Wooldridge (TRW), Sperry-Rand, IBM, Jet Propulsion Laboratories, and other places. If you've ever wondered about the high cost of research, and what the professors were doing with their time, now you have some of the answers:

They were playing around with the odds on the game of Black-jack! If you weren't able to see the results from your tax dollars before, now that opportunity is yours, since these tax-supported researchers are responsible for the calculations that formed the basis for the later work which produced this system.

Perhaps most of the credit should go to Dr. Edward 0. Thorp and his treatise on Blackjack, called *Beat the Dealer,* first published in 1962. Dr. Thorp's strategy was based principally on calculations performed by Julian Braun of IBM Corporation and MIT. Dr. Allan N. Wilson, in his book, *The Casino Gambler's Guide,* also advanced a strategy for Blackjack. By admission, his strategy is somewhat inferior to Thorp's. The trouble with the strategies proposed by these mathematicians is that they are far too complicated for the average layman to understand, not to mention to use. This is also true of all the professional-level strategies published in the '70's, including the Braun Count, Revere, HI-OPT, Uston and DHM counts.

A number of people have been selling Blackjack strategies, mostly through mail order, for some time. The very earliest strategies were closely guarded, private secrets that were released at an expense of thousands of dollars. Various strategies have sold for as little as $2.00 to as much as $2,500 through the mail.

In the course of writing this book, we have reviewed most of the current strategies available. We believe that this is the best one available to the average player at this time. It has passed the test of time since it has been used successfully for more than ten years. The first version of this book was published in 1973 under the name *How to Win at Weekend Blackjack.* It sold over 20,000 copies at a price of $20 or more.

In addition to the mathematics of the system, which has been refined for you into simple strategy rules, the people who purchased the first version have thoroughly proven that this strategy works after extensive and successful play in the casinos of Reno, Las Vegas, and Atlantic City. The practical art of casino play is introduced in Part III. Further, we have collaborated with a Black-jack dealer and professional players who collectively have over forty years' experience to bring you the inside picture as it has NEVER been presented before. These people must remain nameless because they presently are working in the casinos. None of the other systems have presented these most important features. Just knowing the mathematics, without possessing the artful skills described in Parts III and IV, will lead you down one short road: being barred from every place you play. In fact, we can positively state that if you learn the material in Part II, without learning Parts III and IV, we can guarantee you will earn the reputation of someone who is "too good a player." You will not be allowed to play in a majority of the casinos in Nevada. If that is your objective, then be our guest.

Once you learn this system and apply it successfully in the casino, you may very well wish to progress up in the field to Advanced Level Blackjack. If this is true in your case, we suggest you purchase our Advanced Level System as contained in *Winning Blackjack*, the #1 best-seller in this field in terms of gross income. This book is the text for the Stanley Roberts School of Winning Blackjack.

CHAPTER 2

THE RULES OF CASINO BLACKJACK

We are going to assume at this point that you know absolutely nothing about the game of Blackjack. For some of you, this will be a bit of an imposition. However, we would advise that even the most experienced player read this section through since everyone will most assuredly gain new insights from our interpretation of the rules.

The Object of the Game

The player attempts to BEAT THE DEALER by obtaining a total of points equal to or less than twenty-one, so that the PLAYER'S card total is higher than the DEALER'S. Any total less than twenty-one is a winner IF the DEALER busts his hand with a total of twenty-two or more.

NOTE: The emphasis is not on getting the closest one can to twenty-one without going over twenty-one or "bust," the object is to BEAT THE DEALER.

Number of Players

The game has a dealer and generally from one to seven players. From the player's point of view, the fewer players the better.

The Shuffle and Cut

The cards are shuffled thoroughly by the dealer and offered to one of the players to cut. The cut is performed by hand, placing one portion of the deck alongside the other, or by insertion of a joker or blank card into the deck at that place where it is to be cut. In the single-deck game, when the cards are hand-cut, it is normal to *burn* (turn face up on the bottom) the top card. This is usually done in such a manner that the players cannot see what the card is. In the multiple-deck games, where a *shoe* (dealing box) is used, it is normal practice to place the cut-card about three-fourths of the way back in the pack. This signals the dealer at which point he is to begin a new shuffle. Some casinos insert the card as little as one-half of the way back. The closer to the end of the pack the cut-card is placed, the more favorable the game is to the player.

Betting

All players place their bets (usually with the casino's chips) in front of them into a small circle or rectangle directly in front of each player before any cards are dealt. A player may play more than one hand, but must usually place twice the minimum wager if playing two hands, and six times the minimum wager, if playing three hands. The minimum bet varies from fifty cents to $100, although it is typically two to three dollars in most large casinos. The maximum bet varies from $25 to $3,000. Some casinos have been known to raise their maximum, particularly when they think they have a sucker. Some smaller casinos which have only one or two tables may have lower maximums down to $10. The ability to vary the size of the bet is the principal advantage a player enjoys over the casino, as you will soon see. Except on a player's Blackjack, or on an insurance bet (discussed later), the settlement of the wager is made on an even money basis, one dollar paid for one dollar bet.

The Deal

Starting at the dealer's left, each player is dealt a card in turn, then the dealer deals himself a card. Each player and the dealer are then given a second card. One of the dealer's cards, usually his first one, is dealt face up; the other face down. The players' cards are either dealt all face up or all face down. In some casinos, the dealer may not take his second (face-down) card until all the players have finished drawing their cards.

The Value of the Cards

All the picture cards (King, Queen, Jack) count as ten points. All the other cards count as their face value, except the ace which—at the player's option—can count either as one point or eleven points. When a hand contains an ace that can be counted as "eleven" instead of "one," without the total exceeding twenty-one, that hand is referred to as a *soft hand.* Any other kind of hand is referred to as a *hard hand.* For example, a hand containing 10,8 would be a "hard" eighteen. A hand containing ace,7 and 10 is also a "hard" eighteen, since this hand cannot count the ace as eleven because the total points would be over twenty-one (that is, the total would then be twenty-eight). A hand that contains an ace and 7 is a "soft" eighteen but it can also total a "hard" eight.

Blackjack

When the player or the dealer is dealt an ace and a ten value card (King, Queen, Jack, or 10) as his first two cards, he is considered to have a *natural* or automatic winner. When the player receives this kind of hand, he turns over his cards immediately. He is paid when his turn comes, generally at the rate of 3-to-2, or 1-1/2 times his original wager. When the dealer has Blackjack, he immediately collects all wagers except in the case where a player also has Blackjack. When that happens, it is considered a stand-off or *push.*

The Draw

Starting with the player on the dealer's left and following around to the next player, and finally to the dealer, each player may elect to *stand* (draw no additional cards), *hit, split, double down,* or *surrender* his hand, in accordance with the House Rules. If the player "stands" (also called staying pat or sticking), he usually signals this move by placing his cards under his wager. In the case of the face-up games, he indicates "standing" by placing his palm down on or above the table. A player may continue to draw

17

cards to his hand, one at a time, by calling for a *hit* (an additional card), until that player chooses to "stand," or he "busts" (gets a total of cards greater than twenty-one). A "hit" is generally signaled by scratching the player's cards toward himself or, in a face-up game, by beckoning with his finger. When he "busts," he automatically loses his bet on that hand. The player is required to turn his cards face up immediately, and the dealer collects his bet and cards at that time. As you will see later, this is the ONLY advantage the dealer has over a good player. That is to say, should the dealer also "bust" (also referred to as *going broke* or *breaking*) he has already collected the wagers of the players who have done the same. All of the cards played are placed face up on the bottom of the deck, in a rack to the dealer's right or to the rear of the cards in the shoe after the settlement.

The Dealer's Strategy

The dealer does no thinking about the manner in which his hand is played. If his initial hand totals seventeen, eighteen, nineteen, or twenty, he must stand after the players have played their hands. He pays all hands that are greater, collects from all hands that are lower, and ties (pushes) with all equal hands. If the dealer has a two-card twenty-one, a *natural,* he collects from all players not having the same. If the dealer has a total of sixteen or less, he must continue to hit his hand until it totals at least seventeen or busts. He cannot hit a hand that totals seventeen or more. Some casinos also rule that the dealer must hit a "soft" seventeen. This rule gives the house a slightly greater edge. Aside from this variation, there is little difference in the dealer's strategy. Should you ever come across a game where the dealer wins all ties, forget it. You are giving the house a significant 9% advantage!

Player's Options

In addition to receiving additional cards, the player has several options at his discretion which are not available to the dealer. These options are granted in different degrees by various casinos or may not be permitted at all.

The first option is called a *pair split*. If the player has two cards of the same denomination (that is two aces, deuces, nines, etc.), he may choose to turn them face up and put an amount of money equal to his original bet, playing each card as a separate new hand. Although 10's may also be split, some casinos require that they be of the same order (that is, two Jacks, rather than a Queen and a King).* Most casinos consider all ten value cards to be pairs. Except for aces, each new hand is played out separately before cards are drawn on the second hand. Split aces are dealt only one card each, face down, in most casinos. In the case of the other pair splits, should an additional card of the same denomination as the split card come up, in effect making another pair, that card may be split again as a third hand, and so on. Some casinos also have rules as to the number of split hands, such as four hands only or two hands only.

The second option is referred to as *doubling down*. When a player feels he has a good hand with his first two cards, and that it will become a very good hand with one additional card, he may turn his two cards face up, double his bet, and receive one and only one additional card, usually dealt face down. Some casinos only permit this with a two-card total of ten or eleven. Others will with nine, ten or eleven, while many permit this on any two-card hand. When one of the two cards held is an ace, this is referred to as *soft doubling*, since the player has a soft hand initially.

The third option is referred to as *insurance*. When the dealer's face-up card is an ace, some casinos offer the player a side bet as to whether or not the dealer has a ten value card in the hole (making his hand a natural and an automatic winner). The dealer must offer "insurance" before he looks at the hole card (to prevent from giving it away by facial expression). "Insurance" is the most misunderstood option in the game of Blackjack. Most players

---

Two ten-value cards of different denominations are sometimes called a "mixed marriage," a term used in Pinochle.

think that they are insuring a good hand they may have when, in fact, all they are betting on is whether or not the dealer's hole card is a ten value card. "Insurance" is paid at the rate of *two units for one bet*. The player is allowed to bet only one-half of his original bet. In this case, if the dealer has a 10 in the hole (or Blackjack), the player loses his original bet and wins the insurance side bet, thereby retaining his original bet. If the dealer does not have a 10 in the hole, the player loses the insurance bet and must play his hand as he would normally.

The last option available to the player is referred to as *Surrender*. It originated in the Far East, and is gaining popularity with the Nevada casinos, although most do not offer this option at present. Simply stated, when the player looks at his hand and the dealer's face-up card, then decides that he has the worst of it, he may throw in his hand before drawing any other cards, surrendering half of his original bet. In New Jersey, the player may surrender his hand before the dealer checks his hole card. Thus, he could conceivably surrender when the dealer has a Blackjack (before the dealer looks, of course). This rule is called "Early Surrender."* Should the player exercise a split or double down option, he only loses his original bet when the dealer has a "natural." In some European casinos which offer Early Surrender, the player loses all bets when the dealer has a Blackjack. At least one casino in the world, Genting Highlands in Malaysia, has a five-card rule that allows the player to take a win of half his bet if his first five cards total twenty-one or less, before the dealer shows his hole card.

---

*Surrender was removed as an option in Atlantic City in May of 1981. It may be reinstated in the future so we are covering it in this book.

PART II

BLACKJACK AS A
MATHEMATICAL SCIENCE

CHAPTER 3

THE WINNING STRATEGY IN SIMPLE FORM

This part of the text deals generally with the mathematics of gambling and particularly with the mathematics of Blackjack. Other books on this subject have presented tedious scientific explanations on the reasons why their strategies are correct. We shall ignore that aspect and limit our figures and explanations only to those features which will help you to better understand the principles of what is happening in the apparently simple-but-actually complex game of Blackjack.

We caution the reader to remember that the simplicity of our explanation does not signify that the forthcoming strategy was developed with ease. Many years of independent research by some of our top aerospace scientists and mathematicians went into the development of this strategy. Over 9 billion simulated hands were played out on a computer to test this strategy. What remains is a simple statement of each rule for you to learn and follow. We caution you NOT to deviate from this strategy, in spite of what your intuition may tell you or what your limited experience with the system may temporarily indicate. If you play long enough you will see the system work while your bankroll grows.

In this section we will first describe mathematics versus chance in gambling, followed by descriptions of some of the so-called betting systems used in the past by fools and compulsive gamblers. We will then explain the basic fundamentals of how to play each and every hand. A presentation will follow on why and how we count the cards, and there will be a section on learning Basic Strategy.

Mathematics vs. Chance in Gambling

All games of chance deal with the probability that one event will occur versus some other events. This probability is referred to as the odds. Thus, when one flips a coin, the probability of heads versus tails is expressed as the ratio 1:1 or 1-to-1 odds. This means that one out of every two times, in a long series of trials, the coin will show heads. Similarly, the probability of tails is exactly the same. The odds are therefore said to be even.

If we examine a die that is used in the game of craps, we will see that it has six faces, each bearing a different number from one to six. If the die is a perfect cube, perfectly balanced, then the probability of any one number coming up is one out of six trials. The odds against that event occurring are five out of six trials. Therefore, the odds of the event happening are 1:6 or 5-to-1 against.

If you were to run a gambling casino which played this game of throwing one die, and you were to pay off the winners at 5-to-1, you wouldn't lose any money, but would go broke from paying the operating costs. What keeps the casinos open is that they always pay off at something less than the true odds. They keep on collecting this "house percentage" on every bet, and that is how they make their money. Some examples follow:

In roulette, the odds against any particular number coming up are 37-1, since there are thirty-eight numbers on the American wheel (0, 00, and 1-36). The casino pays this bet at 35-1. Therefore, in theory, and in the long run, every time a bet is made on a number, the house is collecting 2/38ths, or 5.26%!

In craps, the odds against rolling a seven are 30:6; that is, there are thirty-six possible combinations of dice, six of which equal a total of seven. Therefore, the odds are 30-(non-sevens) to 6 (sevens) against the player, or 5-to-1. If you bet on a seven being thrown, and seven comes up, the house will only pay you four times your bet instead of five times. Some casinos deliberately try to confuse the player by printing "five for one" on the craps layout. This means that they give you four of theirs plus one of yours for your bet of one. In this case the house percentage is 1/6 or 16.67%.

A similar situation exists with slot machines where the number of the various symbols of each kind on the machine limits the probability of the various kinds of payoffs.

If you bet at the racetrack, you know that the odds are totaled after all the bets are in. The track takes its percentage off the top and divides the rest, by totalizator machine, among the winners.

Independent Trials vs. Dependent Trials

To facilitate your understanding of an independent trial versus a dependent trial, the following example will be used:

Let us imagine twenty marbles (ten white and ten red) concealed from view in a container. If we extract a white marble from the container, make note of this result, and replace the white marble back into the container, we could not make an educated guess as to what the color of the next marble would be if we were to repeat the same procedure. As long as the marble is put *back* into the container, the ratio of white marbles to red marbles will not be changed. Thus, the odds of retrieving a red marble are the same as for a white marble.

The same holds true for the games of roulette, craps, keno and slots. Whatever has occurred previously has no bearing on what will occur next. This means—provided there are no mechanical imperfections—that if one had thrown ten sevens in a row at the craps table, the probability of a seven occurring again would be exactly the same, or one out of six trials. Conversely, had one not thrown a seven in one hundred trials, the odds would still be exactly the same that one would come up (one out of six trials). This phenomenon is referred to as "independent trials process." It is important to understand and even more important to believe this, or you will always have difficulty second-guessing your intuition in a casino.

Let's go back to our marbles in the container. If we extract a white marble from our container but this time keep the marble *outside* the container, we will have an advantage in prediction. We now know that there is a better chance of a red marble being extracted on the second attempt because there are nine white marbles left in the container along with the original *ten* red marbles. This principle of dependent trials, illustrated by this example, is the conceptual foundation for card counting.

It should now be readily apparent that the game of Blackjack can be beaten because it is a game of dependent trials rather than a game of independent trials like keno, craps, roulette, etc. Stated in another way, when as little as a single card has been played from a total deck, the probabilities have been altered until all the cards have been replaced in the deck. For example, when all the aces have been played, it is impossible to get a natural, until the deck is reshuffled. Or, if all the 10's have been played from the deck, one could hit a hand totaling twelve with the certainty that it would not bust.

The knowledge presented herein will allow you to have the necessary understanding to: first, bet a larger sum of money when the player's probabilities of winning are greater; and, second, play your hand in accordance with the best probability of winning. You will, therefore, bet more money when your chances of winning are greater, thereby winning a larger percentage of your big bets and a smaller percentage of your small bets, but your overall winnings will increase. Further, you will know how to make the right decisions on how to play your hand.

CHAPTER 4

BETTING SYSTEMS

We shall now take a little detour into the area of so-called betting systems to show what you should not do and why. Many players down through the years have tried to beat the casinos. Some of these were mathematicians of world acclaim who thought they had developed systems which could recover their losses and ultimately win. If you believe in such systems, you are deluding yourself, just as those poor souls have done. The ultimate proof of their failures is that the casinos are still in business and are more profitable than ever. A plane doesn't land at the Las Vegas Airport that doesn't have some poor sucker on it who has a progressive betting system that he is sure will win. We speak on this matter not as a disinterested observer, but as a once deluded sucker who thought he had a sure thing. These so-called systems are generally categorized as Progressive Betting Systems.

Progressive Betting Systems operate on the general principle that you increase your bet successively to cover your previous loss. There are many combinations for betting like this, and each has its own name. The simplest and most common is known as the double-up or Martingale System. The player makes an initial bet of one unit; if he loses, he bets two; loses again, he bets four; and so on, to 8, 16, 32, 64, etc. When the player finally wins—if he doesn't run out of money or run into the house limit—he wins the amount of his loss plus one unit. Assuming that one was playing Blackjack at a table where the limits went from $1 to $500, one could lose nine hands in a row and then run out, since the tenth bet would require $512, which exceeds the house limit. See the series that follows: (Bet 1) $1; (Bet 2) $2; (Bet 3) $4;(Bet 4) $8; (Bet 5) $16; (Bet 6) $32; (Bet 7) $64; (Bet 8) $128; (Bet 9) $256; (Bet 10)—the one that exceeds the limit—$512. Even if you could make this bet, isn't it foolish to chase that $1 win with a potential loss of $1,023, which is the sum of all ten bets?

Progressive Betting Systems usually insist that a player make the same bet, that is, bet that the same thing is going to occur. This phenomenon is referred to as "betting on a reversal in trend." One bets that something which must happen eventually will occur next, since it hasn't happened for some time. We hope you can see the danger here, as occasionally a long series of one-sided combinations can and is going to occur.

Another less dramatic, but equally foolish, system is the Pyramid, or D'Alembert system. In this system you start with a bet of one unit.

If you win, you start again at one unit. If you lose, you increase your bet by one unit and continue to increase by one unit for each subsequent loss. If you win, however, you decrease your last bet by one unit until you return to the point where your bet will be only one unit. At the end of this sequence, you will have won one unit for each time you have had a win, and hopefully you will not have run out of money before you have recouped your losses.

Another equally foolish system is the number series, or cancellation system, sometimes attributed to the mathematician Descartes. In this system, one writes down a series of numbers—say 1, 2, 3. You then bet the sum of the first and last numbers, or four units. Should you lose, you add the new last number (4) to the first and bet that sum (5). When you win, you cross out the sum (5) and the two numbers that added up to it (1 & 4), and determine a new sum (bet) by adding the first and last numbers (2 + 3 = 5) remaining. If there is only one remaining number, it is rewritten and bet. This continues until, hopefully, the entire series is canceled out. This appears to be an attractive system since one can lose more bets than he wins yet come out ahead. Again, however, the bugaboo of the system player will arise—

that oddball series in which the trend just doesn't seem to reverse. We know from personal experience, that this system doesn't work when an almost impossible occurrence of twenty-three out of twenty-six trials came up wrong (for us), and wiped out our bankroll. We urge you to profit from our youthful inexperience and foolishness, and not fall prey to false promises.

There is simply no betting system that can win for you in the long run, especially when the house pays off at less than true odds. If you are tempted to try these systems then do yourself a service by first playing on paper. If you can twice succeed in doubling your bankroll three successive times, so that you will have twice succeeded in winning eight times your bankroll, then you will have a winning system. If you wish to profit from the experience of millions of others then stop deluding yourself and stop wasting your time. Read on and you will find another kind of system that really works without relying fundamentally on chance occurrences.

Basic Strategy

Many people mistakenly believe that if they play their hands exactly as the dealer must play his, the game will at least become even, if not tip somewhat in the player's favor. (The rules governing the dealer's play in Blackjack are described in Part I.) Such strategy actually works out to a 4-1/2% advantage in favor of the house! What, then, can the average player do to minimize the house's advantage at Blackjack? The answer will be found in Basic Strategy.

CHAPTER 5

BASIC STRATEGY FOR SINGLE DECK BLACKJACK

For reasons that we will explain later, the single-deck game offers the player a far better chance of winning more. This assumes you are, first, playing properly and, second, playing in accordance with the identical set of rules. Therefore, as a beginner, you should concentrate on single-deck play. If the casino you are in does not permit a particular rule, e.g., Surrender, then you go on to the next applicable strategy rule. To best facilitate smooth, orderly play, the player should ask himself a series of questions immediately after the cards have been dealt and the dealer's face-up card is available for all to see. The first question is: "Do I have a SURRENDER hand?"

Table 1

SURRENDER—BASIC STRATEGY (SINGLE DECK)

DEALER SHOWS	YOU SURRENDER
Ace	(10,6)
10	(10,6), (10,5), (9,7), (9,6), or (7,7)

How to determine whether or not a player has a Surrender hand is shown in Table 1. If the player has a 10,6 versus the dealer's ace, this table indicates that Surrender is the proper strategy (remember that all face cards are ten value cards). Likewise, if the dealer is showing a 10, the player must check his hand to see if he is holding a 10,6; 10,5; 9,7; etc. If so, Surrender is his proper playing strategy. If this situation does not apply (if the player is holding a pair of 5's, for example), then the player continues on with his question-asking and decision-making.

It must be remembered that Surrender is not a money-winning strategy per se, but a money-saving strategy. When correctly used, Surrender results in the loss of half the original wager, whereas, without it, more than 75% of the time all of the wager would be lost. It stands to reason, therefore, that Surrender becomes a profitable play in the long run.

If the player does not have a Surrender hand, the next question is, "Do I have a PAIR?"

If a player does have a pair, he makes his playing decision based upon what the dealer's up-card is and what Table 2 indicates For example, if the player has a pair of 9's, he asks himself, "When am I allowed to split 9's?" Table 2 says that the player should split his 9's when the dealer's up-card is a 2 through 9, unless he has a 7. The rest of the table is read in the same way.

(See next page for Table 2)

Table 2

PAIR SPLITTING—BASIC STRATEGY (SINGLE DECK)

YOUR HAND	DEALER SHOWS
(2,2)	3-7 (*2-7)
(3,3)	4-7 (*2-7)
(4,4)	Never (*4-6)
(5,5)	Never
(6,6)	2-6
(7,7)	2-7 (*2-8)
(8,8)	Always
(9,9)	2-9, Except 7
(10,10)	Never
(Ace,Ace)	Always

*Indicates when doubling after split is allowed (DASA)

Some casinos allow the player to double down after splitting a pair while others will only allow doubling on the first two cards dealt. The asterisk denotes those situations where doubling after a split is allowed (DASA). For example, if a player is dealt a pair of 3's, Table 2 says to split them when the dealer is showing 4 through 7. But if doubling after a split is allowed, then the pair of 3's could be split against the dealer's 2 through 7. The player then hopes that he gets a good card (such as a 7 or 8) on at least one of his hands, so that he'll have a good doubling down situation.

For those situations where Basic Strategy applies, pairs should be resplit. If a player splits a pair of 3's, and the dealer places another 3 on one of them, that pair should be split again, and so on.

Aces are peculiar in that they cannot be resplit in most casinos, and only one card is dealt to each. Also, if a ten value card is dealt to one or both of the split aces, the player does not have a "natural," but has a card total of twenty-one. If the hand wins, the player will receive even money instead of the 3-to-2 Blackjack payoff. Nevertheless, aces should always be split.

But if our hypothetical player does not have a pair (or one that he is permitted to split), he may yet have another type of playing hand. "Do I have a SOFT DOUBLING hand?" (A "soft" hand is one that contains an ace and a card other than a ten. For example: ace,6 is a "soft" seventeen.)

Table 3

SOFT DOUBLING—BASIC STRATEGY (SINGLE DECK)	
YOUR HAND	DEALER SHOWS
(Ace,2); (Ace,3); (Ace,4); (Ace,5)	4-6
(Ace,6)	2-6
(Ace,7)	3-6
(Ace,8)	6
(Ace,9)	Never

Table 3 is read in the same manner as Table 2. That is the player looks at his hand and then bases his decision upon the dealer's up-card. When would our player double down on ace,7? He would double down only when the dealer is showing 3 through 6. If our player does have a soft hand but is not permitted by Table 3 to double down on it, he should refer to the SOFT STANDING Strategy in Table 5.

Let's now assume that our player doesn't have a Blackjack (an instant winner), or a hand that should be surrendered, or a pair that should be split (pairs that should not be split will fall into HARD STANDING Strategy or HARD DOUBLING Strategy), or even a soft doubling hand. "What about HARD DOUBLING?"

Table 4

HARD DOUBLING—BASIC STRATEGY (SINGLE DECK)	
YOUR HAND	DEALER SHOWS
(6,2)	Never
(5,3) or (4,4)	5 or 6
9	2-6
10	2-9
11	Always

Again, Table 4 is read in the same manner as the other tables. Our player would double down on his hard total of ten, for example, only when the dealer is showing a 2 through 9 (note that this includes a pair of 5's, a hand that should never be split but often is good for hard doubling). Our player should refer to Table 4 after he's split a pair (DASA) and is contemplating doubling down on one of the hands. If hard doubling does not apply or is not allowed by Table 4 (a hard total of nine versus the dealer's 10, for instance), then the player should refer to Table 6, HARD STANDING Strategy.

Reno Variation

When playing single deck in Reno, ignore the Surrender table and the DASA in pair splitting. Also ignore the Soft Doubling Strategy, and play your soft hand according to the soft standing table with the dealer hitting a soft 17. The only other change will be in the hard doubling table; you will be limited to hard doubling on 10 and 11 only.

Let's go back for a moment to our friend who was dealt a soft hand but is not permitted by Table 3 to double down on it. Let's say that he has ace,6 against the dealer's 7. According to Table 3 he can only double down if the dealer is showing a 2 through 6. What should he do? He should refer to the SOFT STANDING Strategy.

Table 5
SOFT STANDING—BASIC STRATEGY (SINGLE DECK)

DEALER SHOWS	YOU STAND ON
2-8	18
9 or 10	19
Ace	18 (*19)

*Indicates casino hits soft 17 (Ace,6), (Ace,2,4), etc.

Table 5 tells our player with ace,6 versus 7 to "hit" (take another card) until the soft total of his cards is eighteen or greater. Similarly, a player with ace,7 against a dealer's 9 or 10 would have to hit his hand, too, until he reaches nineteen or greater. Same thing with ace,3; ace,4; etc. If soft doubling is not allowed by the Soft Doubling Strategy (or if soft doubling is not allowed, period, as is the case in Reno, Nevada), then Soft Standing Strategy takes over.

As mentioned earlier, some casinos require that their dealers stand on all seventeen point totals while some require them to hit a soft seventeen. It's easy to tell which casinos require their dealers to hit a soft seventeen because it is usually written right on the playing felt of the Blackjack table, just above where it also says, "Insurance pays 2-to-1." In the casinos where dealers hit a soft seventeen, the Soft Standing Strategy against a dealer's ace is to stand on nineteen rather than eighteen. Casinos which do not hit a soft seventeen have "Dealer must stand on all 17's" written on the playing felt.

What if our player is not fortunate enough to draw 3 or 4 on his ace,6, but draws a 5 instead? With a 4 he would have had a soft twenty-one, a probable winner. Now he has a *hard* twelve. The hand is no longer soft; the soft total for ace, 6, 5 would be twenty-two, a bust. Since the hand is no longer soft, he must now (and this is the final and most important series of decisions) refer to the HARD STANDING Strategy.

Table 6

HARD STANDING—BASIC STRATEGY (SINGLE DECK)	
DEALER SHOWS	YOU STAND ON
2 or 3	13
4-6	12
7, 8, 9 or Ace	17
10	17 or (7,7)

This is the most frequently used strategy in casino Blackjack. Pairs come up only occasionally, as do hard and soft doubling hands. To be precise, you will receive a pair 13.1% (14.5% in a four-deck game) of the time, but not all of these hands are able to be used as splits. This information, as well as a host of other statistics about the game may be interesting, but they are not useful to you. That is why they won't be found in this book since statistical data tend to confuse most people and tend to divert your mental activity from the learning process. Rest assured, dear reader, that we have all the numbers. The proven genius of what is offered here is that just about anyone who wants to can learn to use this material.

But more often than 70% of the time, the player is faced with the simple but-not-so-simple dilemma of whether to hit or stand. Table 6 is to be followed in the same manner as the others. When the dealer is showing a 2 or 3, the player must hit his hand until his card total is thirteen or more. Similarly, if the dealer is showing a ten value card, the player will stand only if he has a total of seventeen or a pair of 7's. Remember, if Surrender is allowed, a pair of 7's should be surrendered to a dealer's 10. In casinos where Surrender is not allowed (and they are in the majority), the player should stand on 7,7.

As a general note it is very important that the tables be followed to the letter. In Table 4, the Hard Doubling Strategy, the player's hand of 6,2 is never a doubling hand, 5,3 and 4,4 sometimes are. In Table 6, the Hard Standing Strategy, a hand of 9,5 is not the same as 7,7 (a pair of 7's). With 9,5, the player would hit his hand till he reaches seventeen, while the player with 7,7 would stand.

In Basic Strategy, insurance is a poor bet, and it should never be made. In a single deck of cards there are sixteen ten-value cards and thirty-six cards that are not ten value. This makes the chances of any one being a 10 about 31%. Since insurance is paid at the rate of 2-to-1, the dealer would have to have a 10 as his hole card under the ace 33.33% of the time for insurance to be an even bet. If the dealer's ace and the player's two cards are subtracted from the 52 as non-tens, the percentage is still only 32.6%. Suffice it to say that unless card counting is employed, insurance is a losing bet.

Playing casino Blackjack involves a series of question-asking and decision-making. During *every* hand the player must ask himself strategy questions *in order.* Do I have a SURRENDER hand? Do I have a PAIR? Do I have a SOFT DOUBLING hand? Do I have a HARD DOUBLING hand? Should I stand on my SOFT hand? What does my HARD STANDING Strategy tell me to do?

If the player follows this outline for decision-making, there will not be one hand that cannot be played correctly according to Basic Strategy.

CHAPTER 6

THE BASIC PRINCIPLE OF WINNING BLACKJACK

As we have stated before, the system presented in these pages depends upon the player's knowledge of the remaining cards in the deck for it to function. By knowing what remains, the player can bet with the highest probability of winning the most or losing the least. It is important to note here that we are dealing with probability and not certainty most of the time. One should also be cognizant of the fact that there will be occasions when you will lose the hand, even though you followed the correct strategy. However, in the long run, you will make the most out of your hand by winning a greater amount of money. One should also be aware that certain hands that are held by the player are essentially bad (or losing) hands to start. For example, a two-card total of sixteen is a very bad hand, a probable loser. In these situations, the best one can hope for is to minimize his losses by playing that hand properly. What to do in this and every other case one will encounter has been shown.

Ideally, a person who has a photographic memory could be the ultimate Blackjack player. He would remember everything that had transpired. If he coupled this with a fantastic ability for calculations, he could instantly arrive at the proper playing decision. Since this does not apply to us, and probably not to you, another method is required that we can learn and use. In order for you to better understand the reasoning behind the strategy, a few examples will follow.

If one knew that all the aces were gone from the deck, the probability of getting Blackjack would be zero. This would reduce the player's advantage, so that one should not make a large bet under these circumstances.

A card that favors the dealer is the five, and to a lesser extent the six. Because the dealer must hit any hand between twelve and sixteen, which has a high probability of going bust, a five will improve that hand greatly. When there are few fives and sixes remaining, proportionately, one might make a large bet.

Thus, knowing when the deck is favorable, a condition we call "rich," is the time to make a large bet. When the remaining deck is unfavorable, a condition we call "poor," is the time to make a small bet. When the deck is neither rich nor poor, a condition we call "neutral," we make a cover bet that is more than our poor bet but not as large as our rich bet. How to do this is discussed in the next chapter.

CHAPTER 7

INTERMEDIATE LEVEL COUNTING SYSTEMS

The Five Levels of Blackjack Systems

There are five levels of Blackjack systems that have been created to master the game. These are: Basic Strategy, Intermediate Level, Advanced Level, Professional Level, and Expert Level. You have already been instructed in Basic Strategy for single-deck Blackjack. Adjustments for multiple-deck play are also included in the Charts at the end of this chapter as well as in the Appendix. This chapter will offer you four highly simplified counting systems. By combining one of these with Basic Strategy, you will have an Intermediate Level system. Advanced and higher level systems are beyond the scope of this text. We will, however, describe how they work here.

BASIC STRATEGY is the way that you play your cards all the time regardless of the condition of the deck. It varies with the rules of the game, including the number of decks that are used but is fixed for those established rules.

INTERMEDIATE LEVEL STRATEGIES use Basic Strategy for the play of the hand, but modify the bet to be made based upon information available in accordance with the count.

ADVANCED LEVEL STRATEGIES are usually simple, one parameter counts that are used to modify both the bet and the play of the hand in accordance with the count of the deck.

PROFESSIONAL LEVEL STRATEGIES involve more complex counts which are used to modify both bet and strategy. Before making the bet the count is temporarily modified by a "true count" adjustment of the number of decks or half-decks left to be played. Since most strategies in this class count the ace as "0," (and the ace is an important card in the betting decision, as explained in the previous chapter), it is also necessary in these systems to make an "Ace Adjustment" before the bet. When you have the proper true count, you then enter a matrix table which tells you how to play the hand, depending upon the index number in that table. The player then returns to his original running count for the next decision.

EXPERT LEVEL STRATEGIES involve counting the cards in groups of usually four or more parameters, thus keeping at least four registers going simultaneously. There are a number of complex formulas that are used, depending upon the particular decision to be made. The matrix table is entered with the multi-parameter count and the appropriate formula. The count is applied to the formula and the result compared to the matrix table to determine strategy and betting decisions.

As you can imagine, it is extremely difficult to master the higher level Blackjack systems. Based upon over a decade of experience in this field, I can tell you what percentage of the population is capable of mastering one of these systems. Approximately one person in one million is capable of mastering an Expert Level system. Approximately two percent of the population is capable of mastering a Professional Level system. About twenty percent of the population is capable of mastering an Advanced Level system. Approximately 40 percent of the population is capable of mastering an Intermediate Level system as described herein. About 60 percent of the population is capable of mastering Basic Strategy. All of the percentages that are mentioned above include the higher level category.

Forty percent of the population will never be capable of mastering any form of Blackjack strategy. Now the above figures do not mean that those percentages apply to the level of skill of the Blackjack-playing public. On the contrary, fewer than ten percent of the people who currently play the game for money know how to play properly. There are less than a handful of people who know and can play Expert Level Strategy. About 200 people are currently capable of playing Professional Level Strategy, some

15 years since these strategies were available. About 2000 people are accomplished to a level where they can play error-free Advanced Level strategies. Nearly all of the above people do not play Blackjack as a profession, but they could if they set their mind to it. Intermediate Level strategies are not suitable for earning a living at the game. Even Advanced Level strategies should not be used for this purpose. When I speak of capability above, I am not necessarily referring to intellectual capacity or I.Q. Certain personal traits are even more important in learning to play Blackjack skillfully. These include: desire or motivation, perseverance, discipline, cool-headedness under fire (when playing for real money), and a reasonable level of intellect, particularly the ability to learn something new. Upon these considerations you can now classify yourself and the probable chance that you will make money playing Blackjack. If you do play Blackjack in a real casino, then any improvement in your game is sure to save you money, at the very least. In 1982 the casinos of New Jersey and Nevada combined to win over $500,000,000 from players who obviously did not know how to play.

Four Intermediate Level Counting Systems

Presented below are four counting systems that can be used to adjust your bet. When the deck is favorable (rich), we will make a large bet. When the deck is neutral, such as it is when it has just been reshuffled, we make a moderate bet. When the deck is unfavorable (poor), we will make a small bet. The condition of the deck will tend to fluctuate more with less decks of cards in use. A more detailed discussion of bankroll and betting is contained in Chapters 13 and 14.

THE ACE COUNT. There is one ace for every 13 cards in a deck. This comes to four aces per full deck, eight per double-deck game, sixteen in a four-deck shoe and thirty-two in an eight-deck shoe. What we are looking for is a disparity in the proportion of aces remaining to be played to give us information about the next hand to come. In order to know this we must count the aces that were played and ESTIMATE the number of quarter decks that have been played. Counting the aces played is a very simple procedure. Just add one for each ace seen. You must, of course, keep this total in your head. Also be sure to count without moving your lips as some people do. Estimating the number of quarter decks (13 cards) that have been played is simply a matter of practice. This can be seen by observing the discard tray. In a single-deck, hand-held game and in double-deck, hand-held games you can also count the cards played; however, this can be difficult. One does not have to be right on the money to do this properly, so most people can learn the knack of estimating after a little practice at home with the number of decks of cards being used in the casino you wish to play. The third factor in keeping a count is to know the particular table to which you must refer. In this case we are dealing with Chart 7–1, * Ace Count for one, two, four, six, and eight decks. It is not necessary for you to memorize the entire table, but only that portion of it which deals with the particular game you are going to be playing. For example, in Reno and many places in Las Vegas, the game is single-deck Blackjack. Las Vegas also has one-, two-, and four-deck Blackjack. In Atlantic City you will find, at this writing, principally eight decks; however, there are one or two casinos that have six-deck Blackjack. If you have a choice, always play the game with the least number of decks in use.

So there are basically three items that you must be concerned with in order to keep track of the cards. The first is the particular card you are counting and how many of those have been played. The second is the number of quarter decks that have been played, and the third is the particular chart that you have memorized for the game that you are going to play.

As a beginner, and in practice, even if you are not going to play in a single-deck game, I recommend that you begin with the single-deck chart because you can commit it to memory in just a few minutes.

---

*see Charts at end of chapter

For those people who have trouble keeping a single running number in their head, which is constantly being added to, there is a mnemonic device that you can use that I find very helpful. Most players fuss with their chips while they are playing. Therefore, the act of handling your chips during the game will not be taken as unusual by any of the casino personnel. Use a stack of chips that is in front of you. If you see none of the particular cards you are counting (in this case, say the ace), keep the chips squared up. When you have seen the first ace, move the top chip to the front slightly, just off-setting the rest of the pile. When you see the second ace, move that same chip off to the right approximately ninety degrees around the clock. If you had looked at the first move as being to the twelve o'clock position, this move would be to the three o'clock position. When you have seen the third ace, move the chip downward or toward you, to the six o'clock position. And finally, when you see the fourth ace, move the chip to the left at the nine o'clock position.

When you are playing in a game where there is more than one deck, you simply move two chips when you are dealing with two decks, and three chips when you are dealing with three decks, etc. Therefore, if you have seen five aces in the double-deck game, or in any game where there is more than two decks, you would move two chips to the twelve o'clock position then you would know you must add the four aces of the top chip to the one ace of the second chip to get five aces. Similarly, you would then move both chips to the three o'clock position and that would be six aces, both chips to the six o'clock position which would then mean you have seen seven aces, and move both chips to the nine o'clock position, which would mean that you had seen eight aces. Naturally, when you have to count nine aces, you would move three chips to the twelve o'clock position, and so on around the clock.

Take care not to move these chips in too regular a fashion, or to extend them too awkwardly off the pile so that casino personnel might become suspicious. You may also perform the same feat with alternate stacks of chips so that the pit boss does not see that you are using any particular fixed pattern that might be detected were he to be very alert.

Now look at Chart 7-1, in particular that section that deals with single deck. In the first row of figures, in the central figure, you will see that the top line indicates that one quarter deck has been played. If you have seen no aces and one quarter deck has been played, you would then consider the deck rich. If you have seen two aces, and only one quarter deck played, then the deck is poor. When two quarter decks have been played, if you have seen three or more aces, the deck is poor. If you have seen one or less aces, the deck is rich.

When three quarter decks have been played, if you've seen all four aces, the deck is poor. If you've only seen two or less aces, the deck is rich. Naturally, when four quarter decks have been played, you would have no information because the deck would be reshuffled. In the other charts you will notice a double asterisk. It is really not necessary to memorize any figures from this point on down, because it is not normal for there to be that many quarter decks in the discard pile. Therefore, it is only necessary to know the charts up to the point of the double asterisks.

Although the charts appear to be quite similar, for example, the first three lines of the double-deck chart are identical to the single-deck chart, this is not true as we get into additional decks. So, carefully compare the first three lines of the four-deck chart with those of the preceding single- and double-deck charts. These adjustments have been made because the frequency of aces has less effect when there are more decks of cards in play and therefore we must make an appropriate adjustment. This has been done by the chart for you.

THE FIVE COUNT. Unlike the ace, which is a card that we would like to have available to us, the five is a card that favors the dealer. Therefore, the reverse is true of this particular card. The more fives that we have seen the more favorable the deck is to us.

Your attention is called to Chart 7-2, the Five Count for one, two, four, six, and eight decks. You will note that this chart is actually composed of five different charts. And you will also note that they are quite similar, and, in fact, the reverse of Chart 7-1. If for some reason you decide to switch from an ace count to a five count, it is only necessary to switch in your mind the rich and poor headings, and you will then have the identical chart. The previous comments on Chart 7-1 also apply to Chart 7-2. In particular, it is not necessary to remember any of the chart past the double asterisks.

A COMBINATION ACE-FIVE COUNT. Now we are going to combine both the Ace and Five Counts into one count. This is a matter of adding and subtracting. I do not recommend that you initially start with this count. You should first deal with either the Ace Count or the Five Count in order to get used to the concept of counting in a casino.

Subtracting is far more difficult than adding. In a casino atmosphere, it is more prone to mistakes. Therefore, the other counts are less likely to get you in trouble in a casino. Now in this particular count structure, the ace is given a value of minus one, and the five is given a value of plus one. It is only necessary for you to keep the sum of those numbers in your head, so that if you see an ace, you subtract one. If you see a five, you add one, and if you see one ace and one five, they would cancel out and equal zero. You will constantly be going back and forth across the zero point using this particular count and, therefore, it is prone to error.

Your attention is called now to Chart 7-3, the Combination Ace-Five Count for one to eight decks. It is important to note that the value of rich and poor varies with the number of decks remaining to be played. Determining the number of decks remaining to be played can be done by an estimating procedure. If there are only one or two decks remaining, and you have a count of plus one, the deck is rich. If you have a count of minus one, the deck is poor. If there are three or four decks remaining, you need a count of plus two to have a rich deck, or minus two for a poor deck. If there are five or six decks remaining to be played, you need a count of plus three to be rich, or minus three to be poor. And if there are seven or eight decks remaining to be played you need a count of plus four to be rich, and minus four to be poor. This is a very simple procedure; however, you are cautioned that it can result in errors. You may also utilize chips as a mnemonic device as indicated previously in the ace count discussion. You may do this by simply moving one chip back and forth or around the circle, or what you may do is use two different columns of chips to count the fives and the aces and simply take the sum in your head.

The advantage of this, of course, is that you will have the count recorded on your chip stacks and will be able to recall any possible error you may have made in the summation process.

THE HI-OPT COUNT. The HI-OPT Count was introduced by Lance Humble a number of years ago. It is one of the most powerful simple counts available to any blackjack player. Unfortunately, the count that was presented originally and the other procedures necessary to utilize this count are extremely difficult. For our purposes, we are only going to use the HI-OPT Count to determine when to make a larger bet, and not to adjust any of our playing strategy. This greatly simplifies the procedure.

In the HI-OPT Count, cards are given certain values. These values are either plus one, zero, or minus one. In this particular count, the three, four, five, and six have a value of plus one. All ten value cards, which are ten, Jack, Queen, or King have a value of minus one. And all the other cards in the deck, the two, seven, eight, nine, ace have a value of zero, so you do not count these cards.

With the HI-OPT Count, we are also able to make an estimate of whether an insurance bet may be correct. We will discuss that at the end of this section. Chart 7-4, the HI-OPT Count, one to eight decks, explains the procedure.

When there is one deck remaining to be played, the count of plus two is considered rich, a count of zero or less is considered poor. In fact, regardless of the number of decks remaining to be played in this particular sequence, poor is always zero or any negative count you have.

When there are two decks remaining to be played, you need to have a count of plus three to have a rich deck, and so on down the chart. As you can see, this is quite easy to memorize because the rich point is one more than the total number of decks remaining to be played. It is extremely difficult to use any kind of mnemonic device with the HI-OPT Count because there are so many cards that one must track and the frequency of movement would soon become obvious to a particularly observant casino person. Therefore, one must commit this particular count to memory and practice it. You should be able to play this in the casino without thinking very much about it. This is not a difficult procedure, but it is more difficult than the previous counts that we have discussed and, therefore, it should be learned last.

INSURANCE. In our previous discussion of insurance under Basic Strategy, we advised you never to take insurance. This is true if you are not counting the cards or if you are using a very simple count as mentioned earlier in Charts 7-1, 7-2, and 7-3. However, because the HI-OPT Count keeps track of ten value cards, and although it is not a precise insurance measure, it is a good enough measure for us to be able to take insurance under certain conditions.

Your attention is called to Chart 7-4, which tells you when to take insurance. When there is one deck remaining to be played, and you have a count of plus two, you may take insurance. If there are two decks remaining to be played, and you have a count of plus six, you may take insurance. If there are three decks remaining to be played, and you have a count of plus nine, you may take insurance, and so on down the chart.

If you notice, except for the condition where there is only one deck remaining to be played, the point at which one takes insurance is three times the number of decks remaining to be played. This should be easy to commit to memory. Naturally, you would take insurance any time that you had the count indicated in the column, or had a greater count. If you have a count that is less than the number in the column, then you do not take insurance.

A last word of advice on card counting. It is important that you disguise your activities as a card counter because this is liable to get you barred. You do this first by knowing these particular charts, the ones that you are going to use, extremely well. Second, by practicing in a casino at a lower level of play to start, and third, by not doing certain obvious things such as moving your lips while you're counting, or staring too intently at the cards. The above activities are the ones that are most often used for card-counter identification by casino personnel.

Remember that it is really not hard to count cards. It is just a matter of a little bit of discipline. The methods that we have shown you here can be learned easily and used for very lengthy periods of time in a casino because they will not strain your mind. However, when you begin to play for money, you will develop a great deal of tension as to the outcome and as to your belief in your own skill. This is natural, and you must simply work your way through it until you get to the point where you can do this more or less by rote. When you have reached that point, then you will be ready to play in the casino for large stakes.

The best rule is to do as much practicing at home as you can before you enter a casino. When you enter the casino for the first time with one of these particular count strategies, try to find a very low limit game so that you have little at risk and will not become a victim of your own insecurity, which is very natural when one first attempts to beat the dealer by skill.

Most of the time you are playing, you will note that you are not going to be precisely on the count that you have to reach. Normally, you'll be away from it, one side or the other, and the decision you will have to make will be more obvious to you. It is only those times when you are precisely on the money that you have a borderline situation, and those are the times when you will rack your brain the most and become the most nervous. When you have a very high count, way beyond the point you need to make a big bet, you will find it very easy to do so.

Chart 7-1

Ace Count for 1,2,4,6,8 Decks

SINGLE DECK

Rich	QDP*	Poor
0	1	2
1	2	3
2	3	4

DOUBLE DECK

Rich	QDP*	Poor
0	1	2
1	2	3
2	3	4
3	4	5
4	5	6
5	6	7
6	7**	8

*QDP – Quarter Decks Played
**Deck usually reshuffled before this point

Chart 7–1 *(continued)*

Ace Count for 1,2,4,6,8 Decks *(continued)*

FOUR DECK

Rich	QDP*	Poor
0	2	4
1	3	5
2	4	6
3	5	7
4	6	8
5	7	9
6	8	10
8	9	10
9	10	11
10	11	12
11	12	13
12	13**	14
13	14	15
14	15	16

*QDP – Quarter Decks Played
**Deck usually reshuffled before this point

Chart 7-1 *(continued)*

Ace Count for 1,2,4,6,8 Decks *(continued)*

SIX DECK		
Rich	**QDP***	**Poor**
0	3	6
1	4	7
2	5	8
3	6	9
4	7	10
5	8	11
7	9	11
8	10	12
9	11	13
10	12	14
11	13	15
12	14	16
13	15	17
14	16	18
16	17**	18
17	18	19
18	19	20
19	20	21
20	21	22
21	22	23
22	23	24

*QDP – Quarter Decks Played
**Deck usually reshuffled before this point

Chart 7-1 *(continued)*

Ace Count for 1,2,4,6,8 Decks *(continued)*

EIGHT DECK		
Rich	**QDP***	**Poor**
0	4	8
1	5	9
2	6	10
3	7	11
4	8	12
6	9	12
7	10	13
8	11	14
9	12	15
10	13	16
11	14	17
12	15	18
13	16	19
15	17	19
16	18	20
17	19	21
18	20	22
19	21	23
20	22	24
21	23	25
22	24	26
24	25**	26
25	26	27
26	27	28
27	28	29
28	29	30
29	30	31
30	31	32

Chart 7-2

Five Count for 1,2,4,6,8 Decks

SINGLE DECK		
Rich	**QDP***	**Poor**
2	1	0
3	2	1
4	3	2

DOUBLE DECK		
Rich	**QDP***	**Poor**
2	1	0
3	2	1
4	3	2
5	4	3
6	5	4
7	6	5
8	7**	6

*QDP – Quarter Decks Played
**Deck usually reshuffled before this point

Chart 7-2 *(continued)*

Five Count for 1,2,4,6,8 Decks *(continued)*

FOUR DECK		
Rich	**QDP***	**Poor**
4	2	0
5	3	1
6	4	2
7	5	3
8	6	4
9	7	5
10	8	6
10	9	8
11	10	9
12	11	10
13	12	11
14	13**	12
15	14	13
16	15	14

*QDP – Quarter Decks Played
**Deck usually reshuffled before this point

Chart 7-2 *(continued)*

Five Count for 1,2,4,6,8 Decks *(continued)*

SIX DECK		
Rich	**QDP***	**Poor**
6	3	0
7	4	1
8	5	2
9	6	3
10	7	4
11	8	5
11	9	7
12	10	8
13	11	9
14	12	10
15	13	11
16	14	12
17	15	13
18	16	14
18	17**	16
19	18	17
20	19	18
21	20	19
22	21	20
23	22	21
24	23	22

*QDP – Quarter Decks Played
**Deck usually reshuffled before this point

Chart 7-2 *(continued)*

Five Count for 1,2,4,6,8 Decks *(continued)*

EIGHT DECK

Rich	QDP*	Poor
8	4	0
9	5	1
10	6	2
11	7	3
12	8	4
12	9	6
13	10	7
14	11	8
15	12	9
16	13	10
17	14	11
18	15	12
19	16	13
19	17	15
20	18	16
21	19	17
22	20	18
23	21	19
24	22	20
25	23	21
26	24	22
26	25**	24
27	26	25
28	27	26
29	28	27
30	29	28
31	30	29
32	31	30

Chart 7-3

Combination Ace-Five Count—1 to 8 Decks

Rich	Number of Decks Remaining to be Played	Poor
+1	1 or 2	−1
+2	3 or 4	−2
+3	5 or 6	−3
+4	7 or 8	−4
A = −1		5 = +1

Chart 7-4

HI-OPT *Count—1 to 8 Decks*

3,4,5 or 6 = +1   10,J,Q or K = −1

Take Insurance at a Count of	Rich	Number of Decks Remaining to be Played	Poor
+2	+2	1	0 or less
+6	3	2	,,
+9	4	3	,,
+12	5	4	,,
+15	6	5	,,
+18	7	6	,,
+21	8	7	,,
+24	9	8	0

PART III

THE ART OF CASINO PLAY

CHAPTER 8

PUBLIC CONTROL OF GAMING IN NEVADA

Gambling is "legal" in Nevada and, therefore, the State exercises controls over its operation. This gaming control is vested entirely in the hands of the Governor, because he alone appoints all the other officials.

There are three public bodies involved: The State Gaming Control Board, which is the administrative body; the Nevada Gaming Commission, which conducts hearings and generally acts as the civilian control over the Board; and the Gaming Policy Board (whose stated purpose is to make policy), comprised of all the members of the Commission, plus the Control Board and the Governor. Our concern is with the Gaming Control Board only.

The staff of the Gaming Control Board is separated into three divisions: Audit, Investigations, and Enforcement. The following text is a direct quote from the Board concerning its function.

"The Audit Division is charged both with the conduct of outside audits and financial investigations required by the Board. The audits themselves are intended to verify gross revenue, license fees and taxes reported and paid to the state; to review general practices, procedures and methods of licensing for the purpose of confirming compliance with the rules and regulations of the Gaming Control Board and Nevada Gaming Commission; to conduct special examinations where circumstances may be deemed necessary by the Board, and to assist in the investigations of the Division of Investigations in its various function.

"The Division of Investigations is charged with the investigation of all applicants for a gaming license, including their backgrounds, financial status and the source of their funds. In this program, agents assigned to the division personally follow their cases to any city inside or outside the nation where their leads may take them. All costs of such investigation are assessed against the applicant and do not represent a financial drain on the state. It has been our experience that the most effective control begins at the front door, so to speak, and that vigorous prelicensing investigation is our best safeguard against undesirable elements.

"The Enforcement Division is charged with policing Nevada casinos for honesty, assuring that the number of games and slot machines coincide with those listed on the tax returns, helping to protect the industry from outside cheaters, and generally assuring compliance with specific laws and regulations applying to the gaming industry."

The Board receives, on the average, ten to fifteen complaints per month. These complaints can be filed in writing or made by telephone. When a complaint is received, it is written up, then investigated as soon as the manpower permits. An evaluation is then made, and the complainant is notified of the results.

There are approximately seventeen people who engage in the field investigations and cover all the games and machines in Nevada. There are thousands of table games and tens of thousands of slot machines for these people to supervise. In order to be more accurate about their work load, we should multiply the number of tables and machines by three (as they operate for three shifts). The investigators cannot be expected to work more than one shift a day, only five days per week.

The Board has no stated regulations or qualifications at this time for these positions. However, they seek individuals who have a law enforcement background and a good deal of knowledge about the games and machines. Such qualifications are necessary since the agents are often called upon to act as expert witnesses during court hearings. In order for a man or woman to have this background, he or she would almost invariably have been a former casino employee. Since this is usually the case, it is highly unlikely that any investigator can work for long in an undercover capacity. Most of the time these investigators will do their work as observers, but occasionally they will actively engage in games as players.

It is more than likely that the casino "grapevine" quickly recognizes these agents, and the casino personnel will be on their best behavior when they are around. (In New Jersey, they are around all the time. Each casino has a full complement of inspectors on hand during operating hours, a much better program than Nevada's, although this would not be practical in a state with 200 licensees. Major casinos should have full-time inspectors.)

The Board and Commission represent the only "court of appeals" open to players in the settlement of disputes. Through recent legislation, gambling debts are now legally collectible, either by player or casino, and should now be a potential matter for civil litigation, but the administrative power of the Board does give it potential authority to settle players' claims which the Board deems legitimate. In New Jersey, gaming debts secured by personal checks are collectible.

The Board claims that undercover agents have been so successful that it has had only a few reported cases of casino cheating. Since we have personally witnessed considerable cheating, we doubt the veracity of that statement. However, it is not possible to discern whether it is the dealer alone who is cheating, or if he is acting as an agent for the casino (since he must admit this himself).

The Board has the power to fine (up to $100,000), censure, or even close a casino, should they find that casino in violation of the rules and regulations. Closing a casino is a rather drastic action as it could put as many as 7,000 people out of work. Since 1955, about twenty-five casinos have been closed. Most of these were small casinos. However, the Silver Slipper in Las Vegas, the Riverside Hotel in Reno, and recently The Aladdin in Las Vegas are three of the notable, larger casinos to be closed. The Riverside has now reopened, and the Silver Slipper is now under new management (the Howard Hughes organization), as is The Aladdin.

It would appear that a major casino has too much at stake to cheat the small-time player, since it has the edge anyway and time is on the casino's side. It is unlikely that a player will be cheated at a major casino as a matter of house policy, but this does not stop an unscrupulous dealer from cheating the player for a host of potential reasons (these will be explained in a later section of this text).

The Board keeps close tabs on the books of the casinos through their Audit Division. Casinos that have strong operating balances and good financial records are less likely to cheat than those that may be in trouble. However, this likelihood does not keep the Board from periodically investigating all the casinos.

The Board states that slots are generally set between 5% and 10% for the house, and that keno gives the house greater than a 20% edge. They also state emphatically: "There is no mathematical system possible which will enable the player to beat the wheel."

In the text published by the Board called, *Legalized Gambling in Nevada,* you will find this statement: "Research by the Control Board does tend to indicate that casinos have a 2.5% edge over the player in Twenty-one, but that highly skilled players can reduce the odds to 1% or less." A private discussion with one of the members of the Board in 1971 indicated that the Board knows that certain skilled players (like Dr. Edward O. Thorp, who wrote *Beat the Dealer*) can actually beat the casinos. These skilled players are generally referred to as *"counters."*

Ultimately, the casino is forced to bar such counters from further play, even though they are not doing anything illegal or in bad taste—except, of course, WINNING. The position of the Board is that the casino is in business to make money, and those players who are good at the game of Twenty-one (and are recognized as such by the house) can be barred from future play. Stating this another way, only those players who lose are welcome to continue playing. Card counters may NOT be barred in New Jersey.

Now, let us look objectively at the Gaming Commission to see if it will give your complaint a fair shake. First, we must recognize that one third of all the State's revenue comes from taxes on gambling. Further, a good portion of the remainder comes from taxes on industries such as motels, restaurants, etc., that are only in operation due to the fact that people who have come to gamble also have other needs, such as food, clothing and shelter. If you were cheated in the casino, it would be your word against the dealer's, and he would be backed up by a host of big businessmen who know the Governor and everybody else.

It is our conclusion then, if you happen to be an average individual, your rights will barely be protected when you enter the casino. It simply would be against the best interests of the State of Nevada to close a casino or to have any scandal concerning cheating. The only way that cheating is stopped—and it is usually only temporarily halted—is when a good reporter digs into the facts, and has a courageous publisher who will let him print these facts. By its nature, the Commission and the Board protect the State of Nevada, and not the public in general. This is especially true since most of the "public" in Nevada who need protection are Californians, Texans, New Yorkers, etc.

We believe that the Gaming Control Board tries to do an honest job in keeping the games straight and the mobsters out. But with the limited number of staff available, it is hard to believe that this job can be done adequately. The best a player can do to protect himself is to play only in large casinos and bet modest sums (since, theoretically, there is too much at stake for the big casino to try to cheat a small-time player). Since the recognized, better Twenty-one players are barred, and the rest of the games cannot be beaten mathematically, the only player who can make a profit in the casino is an *unrecognized,* skilled Twenty-one player.

CHAPTER 9

THE CASINO

Enter the glittering and deceptive world of the gambling casino at your own peril. Here you will find excitement and distractions to challenge the eye, distort the mind, deaden the ear, inebriate the brain and gently, sweetly, but deftly, separate you from your hard-earned wages. No wonder Las Vegas is nicknamed, "Lost Wages." All this will happen, unless you heed the advice that follows and precedes this section on the casinos, their owners and personnel.

Like any other business, casinos are owned by individuals, partnerships, and corporations. In the last two decades, many major casinos have been acquired by large corporations and some of these have seized upon the opportunity to gobble up many of these money-making ventures. New casinos have been built by major corporations because this kind of construction now costs upwards of $50 million. Principal among the corporate tycoons was Howard Hughes, followed by Del Webb, Caesars World, Hilton International, Resorts International, Bally, Golden Nugget, Playboy, Kirk Kerkorian (MGM), and Bill Harrah.

As stated in the previous section, one is safer playing in a major casino, and should avoid the small, out-of-the-way places. We shall list those places where playing is recomended, contingent upon the current rules in force. We shall also show you how to evaluate the present rules at each casino in order for you to select the most advantageous places to play. Since there are constant changes in the rules, you will have to do your own research to keep pace with these changes.*

The four major areas to play in are: Las Vegas, Reno, Lake Tahoe, and the newcomer, Atlantic City, New Jersey. Las Vegas can be described as two separate places; Downtown and the Strip. Lake Tahoe is basically two areas; the North Shore and Stateline (South Shore). Reno is the most compact area, with casinos located in nearby Sparks, or a few short miles away in either Virginia City or Carson City. Atlantic City has developed rapidly with new construction proceeding at a frenzied pace. If the wild success of Resorts International and Caesars is any indication, Atlantic City will become (if, indeed, it is not already) the Las Vegas of the East.

Howard Hughes' Nevada Operations control four casinos in Las Vegas and one, Harold's Club, in Reno. With the exception of the Silver Slipper and Harold's Club which deal single-deck games, all the Hughes' casinos deal multiple-deck (mainly, four-deck) Blackjack. Occasionally, you will find one or two single-deck games. The other Hughes' casinos include the Desert Inn, Frontier, and the Castaways. The Sands and The Landmark were sold by the Hughes Corporation after his death. The Sands was returned to the Hughes Organization in 1983.

The Del Webb Corporation owns The Mint in Downtown Las Vegas, The Claridge in Atlantic City, the High Sierra on the South Shore, the Riverside in Laughlin. The Hilton Hotel chain owns the gigantic International, the Flamingo Hilton, the Reno Hilton and is planning a casino in Atlantic City. The MGM Grand, owned principally by Kirk Kerkorian, has recently split into separate corporations (one for films and one for its very successful casino operations). There are MGM Grand Hotels in Las Vegas and Reno, and one is scheduled for Massachusetts when that State enacts casino gambling.

---

*By reading Gambling Times *regularly and* The Experts Blackjack Newsletter, *you can keep up with all changes in the field.*

The late Bill Harrah, well known for his famous auto collection, had two major casinos in Reno and at Stateline, both called Harrah's. Harrah suffered some major losses to early system players and because of that was quite wary of them. Dealers were instructed to reshuffle the deck at about thirty cards in Harrah's. All things considered, he probably lost more money by slowing down the action than by allowing a few system players to win small sums. Holiday Inns has since acquired all of Harrah's properties, and is expanding with additional gaming operations, including two casinos in Atlantic City and the Holiday Casino on the Las Vegas Strip.

The Golden Nugget, directed by young Steve Wynn, has casinos in Las Vegas and Atlantic City. Look for this active group to continue to grow.

Resorts International, as the first casino in Atlantic City, was an immediate success. It operates two casinos in the Bahamas as well.

Caesars World has casinos in Las Vegas, Caesars Palace; Tahoe, Caesars Tahoe; and Atlantic City, The Boardwalk Regency. A fourth casino is planned for Atlantic City.

Bally, the world's premier slot machine manufacturer, opened its first casino in Atlantic City. Although there are no current plans for a second casino, keep your eyes on this well-placed company.

Regional lists of the larger casinos now open and their rules appear on the following pages. You will find these lists (Charts A-F) extremely useful guides for mapping out your playing trips.

How to Read the Casino Charts A-F

All the casino lists (Chart A through Chart F) are to be read in the following manner. The first column is the name of the casino. Column two gives the total number of Blackjack tables in that casino (remember that some or all of the tables may be closed, due to the season, shift or the day of the week). Column three shows the number of decks that are used. For example, "1/6" indicates that both single-deck games and six-deck shoes are available in that casino. Again, this will change due to the time of day (shift), day of the week, season of the year, holidays, and the whims and wishes of the casino managers.

Column four tells you the shuffle point (such as one deck remaining, half a deck remaining, etc.). This will only be useful for shoes, as the shuffle point for single and double-deck games will vary widely, even within the same casino, due to the whims of particular pit bosses, dealers, and the size of your bet.

Column five tells you whether or not the casino offers Surrender. A dot in column five indicates that Surrender is allowed, and an "E" in column thirteen indicates Early Surrender. (Although New Jersey recently canceled Surrender, it may be reinstated.)

Column six shows the casinos that allow doubling after the split (DASA), and column seven indicates the casinos that allow doubling down on hard totals of nine or less. Column eight tells which casinos permit soft doubling, and nine shows whether or not the casino hits soft seventeen.

The house limit for Blackjack is shown in column ten. This would be the maximum dollar amount you could bet on any one hand. This limit may be raised for you if you ask the casino pit boss.

Column eleven tells you if the shoe games are dealt face up or face down. All other things being equal, the face-up games are preferred because they make the counting easier.

Column twelve indicates the number of playing positions available per table. The greater the number of positions, the easier it will be for you to find an empty spot at a table.

The last column, titled "OTHER," is coded in the following manner:

A= You may resplit Aces.

B= A bonus will be paid to you on certain hands, such as a spade Blackjack (Ace of spades and Jack of spades), or 6-7-8 of the same suit, etc.

T= You must have a pair of like 10's in order to split them (10,10 or Q,Q, etc.), as opposed to splitting any combination of 10's.

NI= No insurance may be taken. DO NOT PLAY IN THESE CASINOS when you play the HI-OPT Count.

W= Double exposure.(Dealer's hole card is dealt up. Do not play—they take all pushes.)

E= Early Surrender is allowed (see Part IV for rules on Early Surrender).

3= You may double down on three cards (i.e., you have 2,4 and hit versus the dealer's 6. Your hit card is a 5 and now you want to double down on your hard total of eleven. There are casinos that allow this).

4= You may double down on four-card totals from eight to eleven, or soft four-card hands (if, of course, the strategy so indicates).

CHART A

LAS VEGAS STRIP CASINOS	# OF TABLES	# OF DECKS	SHOE SHUFFLE POINT	SURRENDER ALLOWED	DOUBLE AFTER SPLIT ALLOWED	DOUBLING 9 & LOWER OK	SOFT DOUBLING ALLOWED	DEALER HITS SOFT 17	HOUSE LIMIT	SHOE DEALT FACE	# OF SPOTS AT TABLE	ADDITIONAL INFORMATION
Aladdin	35	2/5	1			●	●		$1000	Up	7	
Barbary Coast	25	2/6	2			●	●		$500	Up	7	
Caesars Palace	54	4/6	1½-2	●	●	●	●		$3000	Up	6 & 7	
Castaways	14	1/6	1			●	●		$500	Up/Down	6	
Circus Circus	66	1/2/4/6	1			●	●		$1000	Up/Down	6	
Desert Inn	30	6	2			●	●		$1000	Up	7	
Dunes	35	1/6	2	●	●	●	●		$1000	Up	7	
El Morocco	4	4	1					●	$25	Up	7	W
El Rancho	30	6	2			●	●		$500	Down	7	
Flamingo Hilton	34	2	1			●	●		$500	Up	7	
Frontier	20	6	2			●	●		$2000	Up	6 & 7	
Hacienda	19	2/4	1½			●	●		$500	Up	6	
Holiday Casino	30	1/2/6	1			●	●		$500	Down	6 & 7	
Imperial Palace	38	2/6	4½			●	●		$500	Up	7	
Landmark	17	1/5	3½			●	●		$500	Up/Down	7	
Las Vegas Hilton	32	2	1			●	●		$1000	Up	7	
Little Caesar's	4	6	2			●	●		$100	Down	7	
Marina	11	5	1½			●	●		$500	Up	6	
Maxim	26	1/2/4	1			●	●		$500	Down	7	
MGM Grand	96	5	2		●		●		$1000	Down	7	
Nob Hill	8	1/2	1			●	●		$200	Down	7	
Riviera	31	2/4	2	●		●	●		$1000	Down	7	
Royal Casino	10	1/2/4	1½			●	●		$200	Up/Down	6 & 7	W
Sahara	40	1/2/6	1			●	●		$1000	Down	7	
Sands	22	1/2/4/6	1-2			●	●		$1000	Up	7	
Silver City	18	1/2/4	1			●	●	●	$200	Down	6 & 7	
Silver Slipper	16	1/4	1			●	●		$500	Down	6	
Stardust	33	1/2/6	2			●	●		$1000	Up	7	
Tropicana	35	4	1			●	●		$1000	Down	7	
Westward Ho	18	1/6	1½			●	●		$200	Up/Down	7	

CHART B

DOWNTOWN LAS VEGAS CASINOS	# OF TABLES	# OF DECKS	SHOE SHUFFLE POINT	SURRENDER ALLOWED	DOUBLE AFTER SPLIT ALLOWED	DOUBLING 9 & LOWER OK	SOFT DOUBLING ALLOWED	DEALER HITS SOFT 17	HOUSE LIMIT	SHOE DEALT FACE	# OF SPOTS AT TABLE	ADDITIONAL INFORMATION
Binion's Horseshoe	24	1/2/4	1			●	●	●	$25,000	Down	5 & 6	A
California Club	15	1/2/4	1/2			●	●	●	$1000	Up	7	
El Cortez	17	1/2/4	1½-2½	●	●	●	●	●	$500	Up	7	
Four Queens	48	2/4	1½		●	●	●	●	$500	Down	6 & 7	A
Fremont	32	1/2/6	2	●		●	●	●	$500	Up	7	
Golden Gate	16	1/2/4	1½			●	●	●	$200	Down	6	
Golden Nugget	35	2/4/6	1			●	●	●	$25,000	Up/Down	7	
Lady Luck	16	6	2					●	$500	Up/Down	7	
Las Vegas Club	27	6	2½	●	●	●	●	●	$500	Up	7	3,4,A
Las Vegas Inn	6	4	1			●	●	●	$100	Down	7	E
Mint	62	1/2/6	1			●	●	●	$500	Up/Down	5 & 7	
Nevada Club	9	2	1		●	●	●	●	$200	Up/Down	7	
Orbit Inn	8	4	1			●	●	●	$100	Down	7	
Sundance	28	1/2/6	1½		●	●	●	●	$500	Up	7	
Union Plaza	28	2/4/5	1½			●	●	●	$500	Up	7	
Western	7	2	1			●	●	●	$50	Up/Down	7	

CHART C

OTHER LAS VEGAS AREA CASINOS	# OF TABLES	# OF DECKS	SHOE SHUFFLE POINT	SURRENDER ALLOWED	DOUBLE AFTER SPLIT ALLOWED	DOUBLING 9 & LOWER OK	SOFT DOUBLING ALLOWED	DEALER HITS SOFT 17	HOUSE LIMIT	SHOE DEALT FACE	# OF SPOTS AT TABLE	ADDITIONAL INFORMATION
Off-Strip												
Ambassador Inn	6	4	1			●	●	●	$100	Up	7	
Palace Station	25	1/2/5	1			●	●	●	$500	Up	7	
Foxy's Firehouse	7	2/4	2			●	●	●	$50	Up	7	W
King 8	7	4	1/2	●		●	●	●	$100	Down	7	
Vegas World	14	1/2/6	2			●	●	●	$500	Up	6/7	W
Boulder Highway												
Nevada Palace	13	2				●	●	●	$200		7	
Sam's Town	27	1/2/6	1			●	●	●	$500	Up	6	
Showboat	24	4	1½			●	●		$100	Down	7	T
Silver Dollar	2	2				●	●		$25		7	
North Las Vegas												
Jerry's Nugget	12	1/2				●	●		$50		6	
Long Branch Saloon	2	4	1			●	●	●	$10	Up	7	
Mickey's	2	4	1			●	●	●	$10	Up	7	
Silver Nugget	12	1/2				●	●		$100		6	
Henderson												
El Dorado Club	12	1/2				●	●	●	$200		7	
Rainbow Club	12	2		●		●	●	●	$50		7	
Winner's Circle	7	1/2/4	2			●	●	●	$50	Down	7	
West World	3	4	1			●	●	●	$25		7	
Boulder City												
Railroad Pass	7	4	1				●	●	$50	Down	7	T

CHART D

LAKE TAHOE CASINOS	# OF TABLES	# OF DECKS	SHOE SHUFFLE POINT	SURRENDER ALLOWED	DOUBLE AFTER SPLIT ALLOWED	DOUBLING 9 & LOWER OK	SOFT DOUBLING ALLOWED	DEALER HITS SOFT 17	HOUSE LIMIT	SHOE DEALT FACE	# OF SPOTS AT TABLE	ADDITIONAL INFORMATION
North Shore												
Cloud's Cal-Neva	25	1/4	1					●	$500	Down	7	
Crystal Bay Club	10							●	$200		7	
Hyatt Lake Tahoe	32	1						●	$500		7	
Nevada Lodge	20	1/2						●	$200		7	
South Shore												
Barney's Club	8	1						●	$200		8	
Caesars Tahoe	67	1/6	1	●	●	●	●	●	$2000	Up	7	
Harrah's Tahoe	151	1/2						●	$1000		7	
Harvey's Resort	69	1						●	$1000		7	
Harvey's Inn	16	1						●	$50		7	
High Sierra	85	1/6	1½					●	$1000	Down	7	
Tahoe Nugget	4	1						●	$200		7	

CHART E

DOWNTOWN RENO CASINOS	# OF TABLES	# OF DECKS	SHOE SHUFFLE POINT	DOUBLE AFTER SPLIT ALLOWED	SURRENDER ALLOWED	DOUBLING 9 & LOWER OK	SOFT DOUBLING ALLOWED	DEALER HITS SOFT 17	HOUSE LIMIT	SHOE DEALT FACE	# OF SPOTS AT TABLE	ADDITIONAL INFORMATION
Circus Circus	56	1/6						●	$500		7	
Club Cal-Neva	36	1/2	1					●	$1000		7	NI
Comstock	17	1						●	$500		7	NI
Eldorado	28	1						●	$500		7	
Fitzgerald's	17	1/2						●	$500	Up	7	
Gold Dust Casino	9	2/4						●	$100		7	
Gold Dust West	8	1						●	$100		7	
Harold's Club	45	1/4						●	$500	Up	7	
Harrah's	90	1						●	$1000		7	
Hilton-Reno	76	1/2/6						●	$1000		7	
Holiday (Downtown)	10	1						●	$300		7	
Horseshoe Club	12	1						●	$200		7	
Kings Inn	10	1/6	2					●	$200	Up	7	B
Mapes	8	1						●	$300		7	
MGM Grand	88	4	1	●	●	●	●	●	$1000	Down	7	
Monte Carlo	12	1						●	$100		7	
Nevada Club	14	1/2						●	$500		7	
Onslow	11	1	1					●	$500	Down	7	
Palace Club	8	1						●	$200		7	
Peppermill	18	1/2/6	1					●	$500	Up/Down	7	
Pioneer	8	1						●	$200		7	
Ramada	9	1/3	3/4					●	$300	Down	7	
Riverside	15	1						●	$200		7	T
Sands	16	1/6						●	$500		7	B
Silver Spur	11	1	1					●	$200	Down	7	
Sundowner	23	1						●	$500		7	

CHART F

ATLANTIC CITY CASINOS	# OF TABLES	# OF DECKS	SHOE SHUFFLE POINT	SURRENDER ALLOWED	DOUBLE AFTER SPLIT ALLOWED	DOUBLING 9 & LOWER OK	SOFT DOUBLING ALLOWED	DEALER HITS SOFT 17	HOUSE LIMIT	SHOE DEALT FACE	# OF SPOTS AT TABLE	ADDITIONAL INFORMATION
Bally's Park Place	76	6	2		●	●	●		$1000	Up	7	E
Caesars Boardwalk	54	8	2		●	●	●		$1000	Up	7	E
Claridge	40	6	2		●	●	●		$1000	Up	7	E
Golden Nugget	57	8	2		●	●	●		$1000	Up	7	E
Harrah's Marina	60	8	2		●	●	●		$1000	Up	7	E
Playboy Club	60	8	2		●	●	●		$1000	Up	7	E
Resorts International	84	8	2		●	●	●		$1000	Up	7	E
Sands	57	8	2		●	●	●		$1000	Up	7	E
Tropicana	76	6	2		●	●	●		$1000	Up	7	E

If you intend to play blackjack to *win*, stop in at the Stanley Roberts School of Winning Blackjack in the city you will be playing and request a casino update. It might also be a good idea to check out your skills while you're at the School. If you are not a graduate of the School, there is a small charge for this service, but it's well worth the expense in the long run. The *best* time to get an *official checkout* is *before* you begin playing with your hard-earned money.

CHAPTER 10

CASINO PERSONNEL

Each casino has its own staffing organization, and it varies with the dictates of top management and the relative size of the casino. The format presented here is typical of most casinos, and will be sufficient to describe the typical jobs.

The head of the organization is the GENERAL MANAGER, who may be the owner himself or a business executive. He makes the major decisions about everything. However, his work usually involves more than the casino, as many casinos are extensions of Hotel-Restaurant complexes.

The casino is generally run by a CASINO MANAGER. Often this person lives on the premises, or regularly has a room put at his disposal. Since he needs time to sleep, he is assisted by someone whose title is generally SHIFT MANAGER. Most casinos have from two to four people who hold this position.

The next group of people may be classified as supervisors. Their numbers and titles vary, depending upon casino size and policy. At the head of these supervisors is the PIT BOSS. There is generally one pit boss per shift, per game (Blackjack, roulette, craps, baccarat). A super casino, like the MGM Grand, may have more than one for each game. The pit boss sees to it that the racks are filled. He supervises the Floormen and acts as a Floorman.

The OUTSIDE MAN is a spotter who looks for cheaters or any out-of-the-ordinary play. Occasionally, he mixes in the game, acting as a plainclothes detective. The counterpart of the outside man is the EYE-IN-THE-SKY, the man behind the two-way mirrors, whose principal job is to watch the dealer to see that he doesn't cheat or act with a confederate. He communicates with the pit boss by telephone. Whenever you see activity on the pit phones, beware—you may be getting close scrutinization. Some system players make it a habit to get up and leave whenever the pit phone rings. TV cameras are taking the place of ceiling catwalks, so the "sky" may turn out to be a monitoring room with several observers and TV equipment that can follow you around the casino and zoom in on the dirt under your fingernails.

The FLOORMAN is the general overseer who watches dealers and players. He settles disputes, and his decision is usually final. These men usually are ex-dealers who have years of experience. It can be said, in general, that these gentlemen are usually not as smart as their typically smug attitudes would lead you to believe.

The DEALER is the key party in this staffing arrangement. His role and actions will be described in great detail in a section that follows shortly.

The SHILL is a house player, usually employed to fill the tables, since many people are too timid to play the dealer alone. The shill plays by a fixed set of rules; he (she) cannot hit a stiff (a hand that will probably break or go over twenty-one such as a hard 12, 13, 14, 15, or 16), must not double, and is usually not paid a bonus on Blackjack. The player can ask the shill to leave if he desires, but should be wary of this action since it would draw attention to the player. The shill, unlike stupid players, will usually show you his hand. If he doesn't then ask him to do so. They are paid about $20 per day, and as such are usually retirees or dealers who are breaking in.

The CASHIER is a highly trusted employee who handles the exchange of money for chips, and vice versa. He or she also assists in the cashing of checks and checking of credit records.

The SECURITY GUARD is generally there for your protection. It is unlikely you will ever be bothered by one of these people, unless you create a scene or refuse to leave, or if you are careless enough to get barred.

Most of the people who hold these positions have rather pleasant personalities. Their jobs entail dealing with the public and making patrons comfortable. Most of the upper level supervisors have worked their way up through the ranks of the casino organization. The rise in ranks above dealer level is based exclusively on personality. The overwhelming majority are not college educated and there is no school for such skills except hard experience in dealing with people.

Overseers

The Pit Bosses, Floormen, Outside Men, and the Eye-In-The-Sky have certain specific duties and responsibilities to look after. Some of the principal points they seek to observe are:

1. Who is a big winner? and why?

2. Is the dealer's rack empty or nearly empty? Where did the chips go?

3. Are any of the players cheating? and how?

a. Are they using paint or daub (marking cards with ink)?

b. Marks and scratches?

c. Bent cards?

d. Switching cards between hands (via a confederate or self)?

e. Are they holding out? Manually or by mechanical means?

f. Does the dealer have a confederate playing at his table?

g. Is a player capping (adding chips to or taking them from the bet)?

4. Is the dealer dumping or sloughing off money to a confederate?

5. What are the identities and mannerisms of system players or cheats?

6. Is a player who increases his bet doing so in accordance with a winnning system he is playing?

When they observe these and any other suspicious moves, they must take action to cease the drain of money on the casino's bank. They generally do it at first by making the player uncomfortable and, if this doesn't work, they ask him to leave. If you ever feel that you are being given HEAT, then quietly get up and leave.

To paraphrase an old expression, "He who plays and runs away, lives to play another day." The overseers are never sure whether you are a system player; they can only guess. If you stay around too long, their hunch will become solidified into an opinion, then into virtually a fact in their minds. If you leave quickly, without a scene, they will usually forget it in short order.

The Dealer

The people who deal the game of Blackjack can be classified into three general groups. The great majority are just working stiffs who deal for a living because it pays them more than they would earn at any other occupation, and it's a way in which they are satisfied to work. Depending upon their seniority and experience, dealers are paid from $24 to $50 per shift, plus their share of the tokes (tips). Depending upon the club and shift, tokes average from $10 to over $100 per dealer, per shift. All tokes are split between all the dealers on the shift. The overseers are not usually included in this.

The second class of dealers are those poor fools who are compulsive gamblers. They stay close to the games because they can't get gambling out of their blood. All are usually losers who can't resist some kind of idiotic, progressive gambling technique, typically one they think they originated themselves, which plunges them into constant and continuous ruin. Dealing affords them the opportunity to be close to other gamblers and close to another game. As soon as they get their paychecks or share of the tokes, they head for a Blackjack table. It is not uncommon to see them playing in their own club immediately after they go off shift.

The third class of dealers may be referred to as "house dealers." These are the ones bucking for points with the pit bosses or management. They may throw (that is, deal) the cards at a player in anger, or insult the players (particularly the winners), in order to make the players feel uncomfortable. They do this, believing they are taking the house's position. However, if they knew better, they would try to make the player comfortable as he lost. This type of dealer hopes to rise in the ranks, but seldom does, because he is the exact opposite of what the pit boss should be. Often this type will try to deal extra fast to demonstrate his proficiency. Sometimes he will deal seconds, letting the pit boss know, just to show how "good" he is. This could mistakenly be the first step in losing his job, for a cheater can cheat the house, too, and, who has a bigger bankroll then the house?

Many dealers first learn the fundamentals at one of the schools set up to teach the subject. There is usually one going on at all times in the Las Vegas or Reno areas. The course costs approximately $250. Ordinarily, these schools are run by individuals who are not associated with any particular casino.

A dealer's first job is as a "break-in" for $12 a day plus tokes. The better jobs, shifts, tables generally go to the so-called "top dealers." These are the ones who have influence with the overseers. They may not be any better or worse than other dealers, but they have established themselves with the upper echelons.

All the dealers must have a police or sheriff's card to work. They are fingerprinted and photographed, and these data are run through an FBI check. This FBI check doesn't guarantee that undesirables won't clear, but it helps keep out known criminals.

About 50% of the dealers want you to win, and 50% want you to lose. Their motives are either to make the player feel better (hoping to get tokes), or to make the pit bosses believe they are dealing "for the house."

The intelligent dealer rationalizes the fact that he has taken your money. He comes to the conclusion that you are out for a good time and can afford to lose. Most dealers think that the player has come to lose, believing that what the player wants is confirmation that things are "out of his hands," that he (the player) is not responsible for his own failures.

CHAPTER 11

MECHANICS

The mechanic is the cheating dealer. He goes by an assortment of names, including: Seconds Dealer, Peek Man, Run-up Man, Deuce Dealer, Roll-over Man, or Turn-over Man, depending on his specialty. This kind of dealer is usually very fast with his hands. He manipulates the cards much faster than the average player can detect.

The larger casinos used to have a mechanic "on call." Whenever a player was running hot, a mechanic was called in to cool him off quickly. This is no longer a house policy; however, these people are working—somewhere. They haven't deserted the profession or skills they worked so long to develop. We will show you how to recognize many of these techniques in the next section entitled "Casino Countermeasures."

Some dealers—against the policy of the house—are dishonest. This type of dealer wants you to lose for one of two basic reasons. The first is that he may be sloughing-off money to an agent or confederate, and needs to win faster than normal from you and the other players so that it will not look like he is losing for the house. The other basic reason is that he wishes to impress the pit bosses and staff that he is winning money for the house in order to hold his job or get a promotion. His techniques are similar to the house mechanic's.

Dealers Who Count

One way the house takes unfair advantage of the player is to employ dealers who can count the cards. When the deck is rich, such dealers would reshuffle. If the deck is poor, they would keep it in action until it became rich.

It is unlikely that you will ever come across such a dealer. The reasons are obvious. First, counting cards, dealing, verifying the totals of each hand, making payoffs to winners and collections from losers, require just too much agility to expect from one human being. Only an exceptional person would possess such abilities. Since a dealer's salary is so low, why should he work at this trade if he could do better on the other side of the table?

Second, most casinos prefer that their employees believe that counting is too difficult. Otherwise, they would realize how simple it is, and would play against the house (at another casino, of course). In effect, the casinos would end up training the people who could beat them. A casino's best bet is to avoid publicity about the fact that the game of Blackjack can be beaten by the average player.

Dealer's Additional Duties

In addition to his regular activities at the table, a dealer is also instructed to observe certain activities at the table. First he must be cognizant of the various forms of cheating that a dishonest player may utilize. Some examples of these are:

1. CAPPING—increasing one's bet (after observing a good hand) by placing additional chips on his original bet, or conversely, removing chips if his hand is bad;

2. HOLDING OUT—adding or removing cards by either palming or by means of a mechanical device generally concealed in his sleeve;

3. SWITCHING—two or more players switch cards between each other to form better combination hands...one person usually distracts the dealer when this happens;

4. MARKING THE CARDS—this is generally done with paint or daub which may be sensitive to the cheaters glasses or contact lenses; or cards may be marked by scratching, scoring, shaving,

bending or crimping them (marking just a few key cards might be sufficient).

Dealers are also cautioned to be aware of big winners since they threaten the house's profit. They may be on the lookout for winning system players, who might be detected by their betting patterns, or by the unusually close attention they pay to all the cards. The latter behavior, which may be noticeable because of the system player's eye movement, is only a guess on the part of the dealer and usually requires something else for verification. Nevertheless, the system player must be casual if he wants to be effective for prolonged periods of time.

Player Recognition

One thing a regular system player does not want is recognition by the dealer or house. Therefore, one must attempt to remain anonymous, or get them to mistakenly identify him as a non-system player, a loser. The latter is by far the most difficult of guises, so the player should probably do his best to remain anonymous.

There are a number of ways that the dealer might recognize a system player. These include:

1. His or her facial appearance (including glasses and hairstyles);

2. Mannerisms of a pronounced or unusual nature;

3. Hands (including rings and scars);

4. Clothes (including unusual styles or colors);

5. Conversation—avoid talking with the dealer, particularly about yourself or anything out of the ordinary (but don't be rudely silent);

6. Patterns (returning at the same time and place to the same casino and/or dealer).

The more one repeats the image one presents and reinforces that image, the more likely he is to be remembered.

The Dealer's Confederate

Dishonest dealers, working for the house or themselves, often employ another person who acts as a player. That actor is known as the dealer's confederate. Ordinarily that confederate will sit in the last position (3rd base), but occasionally he will be found at another position.

When a dealer is cheating the player, he will use the confederate (who may be a house shill) to take a card that he does not wish to draw himself. This is typically the act of a dealer who can peek, but cannot deal seconds because he lacks the handling ability. When a dealer is cheating the house, he may use his confederate for a number of purposes. One method is to pay the confederate more than he is entitled to, or to pay him even when he loses. This is popularly referred to as "dumping." A second method is to signal what his hole card is. This can be done when the dealer looks at his card those times when he has a 10 or ace up, or he can peek at it while dealing. If the confederate knows the value of the dealer's hole card, he can play his own hand to better advantage. A third technique is to signal what the card coming off the top is (which he peeked at beforehand). Signals can be given by hand or by facial gestures which are undetectable by anyone except the confederate.

Another method is for the dealer to actually play the confederate's hand. This implies that the dealer knows both his own two-card total and the player's hand. In the multiple-deck games, where all cards are dealt face up, this technique is particularly advantageous.

Occasionally, a dealer who is honest will tip off the player in a face-up game. He may do it by hesitating or by inadvertently playing the player's hand automatically.

Instructions From the House

Like any employee, the dealer is instructed by his supervisors regarding the manner in which he is to perform his job. These instructions usually include:

1. The shuffle point—how far into the deck he should usually deal;

2. What to observe closely—including capping and other forms of cheating;

3. Special reshuffling instructions—when a big jump in bet size is made, or if a new player enters the game with a large bet;

4. Calling out large bets;

5. Calling out when changing large bills, changing chip denominations, and "money plays" (when there is no exchange for chips).

CHAPTER 12

CASINO COUNTERMEASURES

Casinos will do anything they can to stop the system player. We will refer to such activities as Casino Countermeasures, which can be either honest or dishonest. (Knowledge, observation and individual disguise are the player's best counter-countermeasures.) In the following section, we will discuss honest countermeasures, dishonest countermeasures, and how to avoid being cheated.

Honest Countermeasures

Frankly, we find it hard to countenance the concept that there is such a thing as an honest countermeasure. If a game is open to the public and all are allowed to play by a stated set of rules, then we think that the house must accept all the players, good and bad alike. Apparently, the house only wants bad players from whom they can take money. Somehow what the casinos preach and what they practice just don't ring true. The casinos want the public to think that Blackjack is a game of chance. We know it is a game of skill.

In Nevada, the ultimate casino countermeasure is to bar a player from playing Blackjack in that club. If the casinos did this to everyone who won, or to too many good players, the suckers would soon realize that is what they are, and the game and casino profits would quickly die.

A popular countermeasure is to "Break the Deck," or reshuffle the cards. This might be done whenever a large bet is made, or if the dealer has been counting. Breaking the deck too often slows down the game and the casino's rate of profit. It really doesn't pay to do it against small-time players, as the overwhelming percentage of players are losers, and the house may be cutting its profits by a larger figure than they save from stopping the occasional system player. Dealers who count—if there really are any—must be in violation of the Gaming Control regulations, as they are then conducting a game "which tends to alter the normal random selection of criteria which determines the results of the game."

Some casinos believe that fast dealers will discourage system players. If a person is using a difficult system, this may be so. If the player is a novice or slow, he will be confused by a fast dealer. However, a fast dealer is a boon to the good system player because there is no dealer who can deal fast enough to stop the practiced pro. The faster the dealer, the greater the number of hands, and consequently, profit per hour. If the dealer is too fast for you, just take your time in playing your hand.

Changing the deck frequently is a legitimate countermeasure that makes it difficult for cheating players to mark the cards. Some people remark that the deck is "hot" or "cold." This is just a gambler's superstition.

In the mid-Sixties, after the publication of Dr. Thorp's episodes, the casinos tried to change the rules of the game. Their changes resulted in a considerable loss of player interest and the near-abandonment of Las Vegas. They quickly changed the rules back. The various rules do give the system player an advantage, if he knows how to use them.

Although the options afforded the player can be used to his advantage, the poor player usually uses them to his detriment. A poor player splits, doubles and takes insurance at the wrong time, thus increasing the house's percentage. The number of people who know the proper use of the Surrender rules is probably less than 4,000. The original (1971) version of *WINNING BLACKJACK* was the first to publish a Surrender Strategy. As long as there is a preponderance of suckers, the casinos are better off not upsetting the applecart, but rather leaving things the way they are. Their best bet is to try to spot the system players, then quietly bar them from further play. A better policy would be to restrict suspected counters to a low maximum bet (for example, $50). This would allow the counter to win a small amount, and it would encourage the non-counter to play more. Of course, he would also lose more.

Dishonest Countermeasures

Another word for this phrase is cheating. There are two basic forms. The first involves the use of devices; the second requires sleight-of-hand. The former type is not likely to be found in the larger casinos, as its capture by the Gaming Control Board constitutes *prima facie* evidence of cheating, and would surely involve a large fine or loss of license. Sleight-of-hand is far more difficult to prove. It is here and gone, like a flash of light, and its existence is difficult to prove without a camera—and cameras are forbidden in the casino. How convenient!

One way the casino can cheat the player is by removing cards from or adding cards to the deck. By removing 10's and aces, or adding 5's, 6's, and other small cards, the deck can be made to yield a higher advantage for the dealer. This is a dangerous move, since the deck could be seized by the Gaming Control Board as evidence.

In multiple-deck games where a shoe (dealing box) is used, it is possible to rig the shoe to facilitate dealing seconds. This, too, is a dangerous practice for the casino to engage in, since it is clearly a deliberate attempt to cheat.

A clever dealer may have the ability to STACK THE DECK. In order to accomplish this feat, first the dealer has to stack the deck, then make a false shuffle and nullify the player's cut. An exception is when the dealer stacks the discards and turns the deck over before dealing.

One popular form of deck-stacking is referred to as the HIGH-LOW STACK. An example of this is shown in Photo #1. In this situation the order of cards is stacked so that every other card is high and the other low. The power of this is twofold. If the dealer can arrange it, the player will get two low cards. If the dealer knows where the cards are, then he can deal seconds, as required, without having to peek at the top card.

Photo #1—A High-Low Stack

If you wish to see how powerful this arrangement is, stack a deck yourself using 9's, 10's and aces as high, and 2 through 7 as low. Ignore the 8's for the moment. Now deal so that the player gets the low-low cards and the dealer the high-high cards. Play the hand out normally. If the dealer should get high-low and the player high-low, then deal seconds to the dealer or player, as appropriate.

Of course, the tell-tale giveaway in the deck-stacking game is the manner in which the cards are picked up. If you see any unusual arrangement of the discards by the dealer, watch out for a stacked deck. The dealer should pick up the cards one at a time from each hand. If he picks up several hands at once and appears to be rearranging the order, beware—grab your hat and leave.

Another form of stacking the deck is called the KENTUCKY STEP-UP. An example of this is illustrated in Photo #2. The cards are arranged as follows: 7,8,9,10,10,J,Q,K,A. This stack was invented by a dealer in Newport, Kentucky, from where it gets its name. If cards are dealt from this stack to one player, the dealer will win the first two hands; to two players he will win the first round and have an ace for the second; to three players he will win the round from all. When the deck is lying face up on an open table, glance through it for this distribution before you sit down to play.

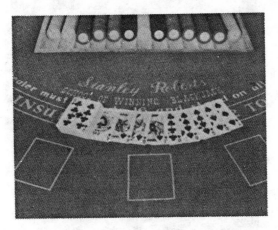

Photo #2—The Kentucky Step-Up

Another little device is to get all of the 10's up front for the first few hands. By doing so, everyone will get a total of twenty, and push with the dealer. But the remainder of the hands will be played from a ten-poor deck.

In order for the stacking dealer to preserve his handiwork, he must execute a false shuffle. One procedure that is utilized is called the RIFFLESTACK (see Photo #3). Although the deck is shuffled, a slug of cards which had been stacked is preserved and kept whole. This slug may be on the top, as illustrated, or at the bottom, which makes it more difficult to detect.

Photo #3—The Riffle Stack

Another false shuffle is called the PULL THROUGH, illustrated in Photos #4 and #5. The cards are shuffled in an angular manner, as shown in Photo #4. They are then pulled through each other, as shown in Photo #5. This sleight-of-hand makes it appear as though the cards are being shuffled, but they are not.

Photo #4—The Pull Through—First Step

Photo #5—The Pull Through—Second Step

After the dealer makes a false shuffle to preserve his stack, he then must get that stack to the top of the deck. He does this by nullifying the cut made by the player. He does this by *crimping, hopping,* or the *turnover.*

The CRIMP or BRIEF, as it is referred to by dealers, serves to set the deck at a particular place. Crimping is done by bending the cards in an arc, or by leaving a few cards askew, and it usually is done in the middle of the deck (as illustrated in Photo #6). The player will generally cut the deck in the place indicated by the crimp. When the player cuts where the dealer sets him up, then there has been no effect from his cut, and it is nullified.

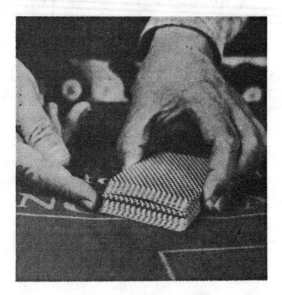

Photo #6—The Crimp or Brief

A dealer who has fast hands may use one of the HOPS to return the deck to the position he desires. Wherever the player cuts, such a fast dealer can return the deck to its original, stacked condition. In the ONE-HAND HOP, as shown in Photo #7, this entire procedure takes place in one quick motion within the dealer's hand. In the TWO-HAND HOP, as shown in Photo #8, the dealer uses one hand to hide his move and assist in the transfer of positions.

Photo #7—The One-Hand Hop

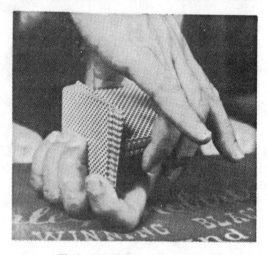

Photo #8—The Two-Hand Hop

This is made to look as though he is picking up the deck in one hand and passing it to the other for dealing. This kind of move should not be construed as normal, since dealers almost always pick up the deck with the hand that ordinarily holds the deck (the left hand for right-handed dealers).

A third type of hop is called the TABLE HOP (illustrated in Photo #9). The dealer uses the table to assist him in the leverage he needs to transfer the position of the cards.

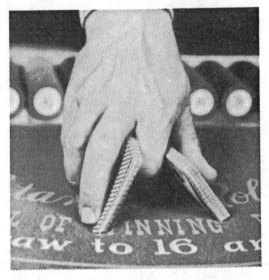

Photo #9—The Table Hop

Another way of cheating players is to stack the discards, then place them on the bottom and turn the deck over. This is appropriately called the TURNOVER and is illustrated in Photo #10, the way it is done with one hand.

If you think the cards that are dealt are the same ones that you played in the last hand, then you may be a victim of the turnover.

Photo #10—The Turnover Being Executed

The principal way that cheating takes place at the Blackjack table is by the dealing of SECONDS. Someone who deals seconds simply takes the second card from the deck instead of the first or top card. If you would like to know the value of this cheating play, deal a few hands as the dealer against an imaginary player. Whenever the top card is not suitable in your hand, take the next one. You will soon see how powerful having this choice is.

In order to utilize the technique of dealing the second card, first the dealer must know if the top card is one that he doesn't want, or if it is a beneficial card. He finds out by "PEEKING" at the top card. There are three basic kinds of peeks. The FRONT PEEK is done with his palm downward, his hand toward the front, as shown in Photo #11.

The top card is crimped so that a corner is visible. This is executed in such a manner that only the dealer can see the card.

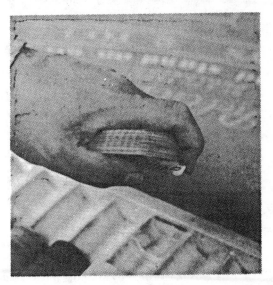

Photo #11—The Front Peek

The BACK PEEK, as shown in Photo #12, is done with the palm in a vertical position. The hand may be held in front, but it is usually toward the side. The thumb is used to raise the card as shown in the photo.

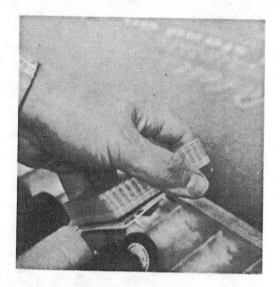

Photo #12—The Back Peek

The TILT PEEK is performed by slipping the top card slightly forward and leaning it up by placing pressure on the front edge. If the deck is held tilted forward, it is not necessary to tilt the card in as pronounced a way as shown in Photo #13.

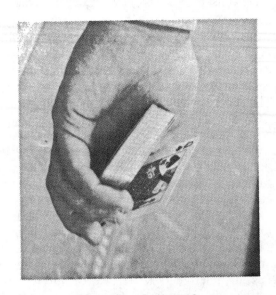

Photo #13—The Tilt Peek

Some dealers use a "shiner" to peek at cards. This is a small reflective surface or mirror that is generally concealed at the edge of the table, or is on top in a place like a pipe bowl. The top card is slid partially off the top of the deck and may be viewed in the reflected surface. In this manner, the deck does not need to be turned over or sideways.

Another method of knowing the value of the top card is for the cards to be marked, which can be done in a number of ways. The cards can be marked with paint or daub; they may be scratched or bent; or they may actually be printed by a manufacturer of marked decks. The best way to detect a marked deck is to riffle the stack at rapid speed, while keeping your eyes on one section of the pattern. If you note any variations, the deck is marked. You will not ordinarily get the chance to riffle the deck in a casino;

however, it is unlikely that a casino would use marked cards, because this constitutes *prima facie* evidence of cheating.

After the peeking dealer sees the top card, and he decides he does not want it, he must find some way of either getting rid of it or taking the next card, the SECOND CARD. One way to avoid the top card is to give it to a confederate who is sitting on third base. This confederate is usually referred to as an ANCHOR MAN. The dealer signals him to take the card, or just deals it to him. If you observe the man on third base making unusual plays, it's time to leave. A second way to avoid taking the top card is to take the bottom card. This is done by turning the deck over, as explained previously.

If a dealer is a real craftsman, however, he is able to deal the second card without trouble and without detection. In order to deal the second card, the deck must be held in a particular way. This is referred to as the MECHANIC'S GRIP, shown in Photo #14. The corner of the deck is held between the index and middle fingers. The thumb is held in a more or less rigid position, which is usually referred to as the "dead thumb." When a dealer (non-cheating type) deals the cards, he pushes the top card forward with his thumb. The second-dealer must hold the top card in place rigidly with his thumb. A dealer who does not deal seconds will usually place all his fingers along the side of the deck, rather than placing his index finger in the front. When dealing seconds, the thumb is used to move the top card slightly, so that the edge of the second card is exposed. Then, by holding the top card firm, the second card is dealt (see Photo #15). The finger is used to keep the third and fourth cards in position. An expert moves the deck so slightly that only a professional can detect his moves.

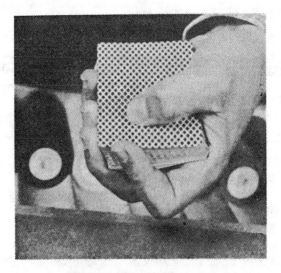

Photo #14—The Mechanic's Grip

Photo #15—The Second Card Being Dealt

How to Avoid Being Cheated

There are a number of techniques which will assist you in avoiding cheaters. No system can win against a stacked deck or a mechanic. Therefore, you must avoid the cheating dealer to the best of your ability. You can do it by possessing knowledge of what to look for, being watchful of what the dealer is doing, discouraging the casino from cheating you (by not appearing to be a winner), and regularly moving (to limit the effect of any cheater on your bankroll).

One of the best ways to avoid being cheated is to look like a loser. The casino has nothing to fear from the average player, so it is normally satisfied to win from him at the typical rate of loss. Concealing your winnings will be described in the following section, "Bankrolling Your Play."

We have already cautioned you against playing in out-of-the way casinos, bars, or private games. Select your casino carefully. You will usually be safe in the larger casinos. Always play at a well-lighted table. Try to avoid the tables that are close to sources of loud noise, although you will never find a really quiet area in any major casino. If you can hear the sound of the cards being dealt distinctly, that is a sufficiently low level of noise.

Observe what is occurring, but also be casual about the manner you use to observe. Avoid suspicious looks or unnecessary stares. A dirty look may be effective in business or personal relationships; in the casino it will probably antagonize someone who may be tempted to cheat you. If you are not satisfied by what you see, then move to another table—or another casino.

If a partner or spouse is assisting you, he or she can be the one who pays careful attention to what is going on while you concentrate on the game. If you are seen in the constant company of another person, this pattern may tend to identify you and ruin your anonymity. You should be cautious about having an associate accompany you on a regular basis to the same places. THE CASINOS ARE WARY OF PEOPLE WHO PLAY TOGETHER IN TEAMS.

If the dealer does anything to make you feel suspicious—even though you cannot put your finger on it—assume he is doing something to your disadvantage. You should be particularly suspicious if there is more than one incident of a similar nature. If cards are incorrectly dealt and strange things seem to be happening with the hands, assume the worst—unless you know that the dealer's fumblings are due to the fact that he is a break-in or new dealer who has no card-handling experience. Be particularly wary of the "old man" who has apparent difficulty in dealing.

Be aware of deliberate attempts to distract your attention by the dealer, floormen, dealer's potential confederate, or shill. They may be trying to get your attention so that the dealer can peek or deal seconds. It isn't necessary for the dealer to cheat you continuously to restore the edge the house has lost due to your superior skills. Once in a while may suffice, especially if you have just made a large bet.

Watch the way the cards are picked up. If you notice a small card being slipped between a pair of high cards, instead of being picked up in the natural order, there is a good possibility the dealer is making a high-low stack. Get a good look at the way the cards are spread out at an empty table. They may be stacked with a Kentucky Step-Up, or a High-Low Stack, or all the 10's may be toward the front or the rear.

Look for the false shuffle explained earlier and illustrated by photographs. Be wary of an incomplete shuffle. The dealer is specifically taught to shuffle the cards thoroughly. If a large batch of cards is left unshuffled, beware of a stack. If the dealer suddenly shuffles the cards in the middle of a hand without having run out of cards, he is probably cheating. This means that he has seen the top card and doesn't wish to give it to a player or take it himself, whatever the case may be. He usually cannot deal seconds, so he achieves the same effect by reshuffling. This practice is expressly forbidden and should be called to the attention of the floorman. He should pay your bet.

If you are adept at counting cards, you may be able to detect a short deck. A short deck is one with some cards removed. It is dangerous though for a player to even imply cards are missing, because this indicates that he is able to "count" the cards in the deck. A single deck with extra small cards is a foolhardy practice for any casino, since the extra card is liable to appear with its duplicate. Deleting a card is far easier, since only the most observant player will be aware of this move. The fact that the deck is spread on an open table—even a new deck that is in order—does not prevent the dealer or house player from secreting one of the cards.

Watch the backs of the cards as they are dealt. Notice if the top card is moving. Observe the border (on decks that have borders) at the edge at the dealer's right hand. If this fails to move very much, you may be a victim of a second-dealer. Beware of the dealer who tilts the rear of the pack backward so far that even a standing "kibitzer" cannot see the top of the deck. He may be trying to keep anyone from observing him deal seconds.

Listen to the sound of the cards being dealt. The card coming off the top of the deck has a distinctly different sound than a second card. If you can hear the scraping sound of a second rubbing against two cards, instead of the swish of the top card, you are in an unusually quiet casino. Make it even quieter by taking your noise elsewhere.

Observe the way the deck is held. Be wary of the mechanic's grip described earlier. Look for any suspicious moves. Look for possible shiners concealed on the table or in an object on the table. In the better clubs in the Reno-Tahoe area, many of the female dealers have been taught to flip the top card from the front of the deck, which looks similar to the tilt peek, illustrated earlier in this text. This kind of move makes second-dealing almost impossible. When you see this move you can probably rest assured that you are not being cheated by a second-dealer. However, if this move is interspersed by two-hand dealing, you may be the victim of a tilt peek.

In order for the dealer to take advantage of dealing "seconds," he must first peek at the top card. Watch the dealer's eyes. If he looks down at the deck too often, he may be peeking. Although it is best to have another observe his eye movements, use caution with associates. If the cards are marked, he only need see the back of the cards to know. The dealer should look at his hole card only if an ace or 10 is his up-card. If he looks with something else up, beware, beware, beware!!!

Occasionally, the dealer will do something that the skillful observer can note and use to his advantage. When the dealer has an ace up, he should offer insurance. He may, by his mannerisms, be trying to offer advice to one or all players as to whether or not he already has Blackjack and therefore insurance is a certain winner, or conversely, that he does not have Blackjack and insurance is a bad bet. If you can decipher his intentions and mannerisms, you will have a most valuable ally. Be sure to toke this dealer as we need him around.

Occasionally, the dealer will try to fool you into taking insurance. Usually he will do this by taking more-than-average-time to give you an opportunity to buy. You must first analyze the dealer's intentions before trusting your judgment. But, even if you guess wrong, you should only be fooled once by this gambit.

One tip an observant player may use to his advantage is the manner in which the dealer observes his hole card when an ace or 10 is showing. If the dealer has an ace up, he is looking for a 10 in the hole. If he hesitates more than normal, or must bend the corner of the card up more than usual, he probably has a high card (7,8, or 9) in the hole because he had to look more carefully to see if it was a 10. If he looked quickly, he may have seen the card was low and that he did not make a "natural." When the dealer has a 10 up, he is looking for an ace in the hole. He will have to bend the card up a little more or hesitate a little more if the hole card is a lower value one, as it might be an ace. If the hole card is a large value, he will see it immediately, and not bend the corner nor hesitate as much.

Perhaps the best way to avoid being cheated is to regularly move around. This will give you the added bonus of being less familiar to dealers and floormen. Never permit yourself to lose more than 10% of your bankroll at any one table. If and when this occurs, get up and leave. You may have been cheated.

Keep records of your activity in a form similar to the one shown in Chart G at the end of this chapter. This will let you know which dealers to favor and which to avoid. It will also help you to schedule your activities. Go back to the tables where you have won and avoid the dealers to whom you have lost. As a general rule you should not play more than half an hour at a table nor more than one hour in a casino, on any one shift. Naturally, a large casino like Caesars Palace can stand three separate tables per shift, while a smaller casino may only be good for one table.

Chart G and Table 7 should be self-explanatory, except for the column marked "Table Time" in Chart G. This column should be used to register the amount of play you got, *not* how long you were at a particular table. To compute table time, take the amount of time at the table and multiply it by the multiplier in line with the "# of other players" at the table (the number of other players will probably be an average). For example, if you played for forty-five minutes at a table with three other people, your table time would be forty-five minutes times .60, which equals twenty-seven minutes.

Table 7	
Conversion of Table Time	
PEOPLE (Other Than Yourself)	X (Conversion Factor)
0	1.00
1	.85
2	.70
3	.60
4	.45
5	.40
6	.33

CHART G

CASINO ACTIVITY LOG

| NAME OF CASINO | TOKES | DATE | # DECKS | TIME | | #OF OTHER PLAYER | TABLE TIME | DEALER | | MONEY | | | TOTAL TIME | COMMENTS AND REMARKS (MAX BET) |
				START	STOP			NAME	DESCRIBE	WON	LOST	TOTAL		

CHAPTER 13

BANKROLLING YOUR PLAY

This chapter deals with what it's all about—MONEY. How much you need to start and how to use it are the subjects of this section. We also discuss the critical factor of the Gambler's Ruin Problem. This will be explained in the pages that follow.

What Is a Bankroll?

Basically speaking, a bankroll is the *total* amount of money that you will commit to Blackjack play for an extended period of time. It is not the amount that you will wager, nor is it the amount you will be carrying around with you from casino to casino. It is the total amount of money that *could* be used, if it were necessary.

The principle that one must rigidly exercise in casino play is: NEVER play with scared money. This means that you should never play with money that you cannot afford to lose. The psychological effect of playing with scared money is such that most of the benefits of the system will be nullified. The frightened player makes mistakes, gives himself away as a system player, fails to act boldly when he should, thus reducing his proper percentage plays.

Always keep your living expenses separated from your playing bankroll. Never try to use your bankroll for daily living expenses. Only use money that you have deemed excess—money that you can afford to lose. This will usually be savings of some sort that you have managed to accumulate beyond your normal needs.

Once again: Bankroll money is NOT next month's car payment or your wife's birthday present money (!), and it is certainly NOT your emergency money. You must provide for these things first so that you will be able to play coolly and confidently. Lastly, bankroll money ought to be considered speculative money that could grow very quickly into a sizable sum, given a sufficient amount of time and correct play.

Gambler's Ruin

There will be times when you will not lose one single hand out of twenty. You will seem to be unbeatable. Likewise, there will be times when it will seem like you should have stayed in bed! What gamblers call "streaks" are nothing more than backward glances at probability to a mathematician. They can and will occur during any short-term period. To prevent a bad series from wiping out your bankroll you will have to exercise self-control and rigidly follow proper bankrolling rules.

One of the best ways to avoid Gambler's Ruin is to divide your bankroll into ten equal parts, each of which is called a "mini-bank." At NO time will you permit more than one of these mini-banks to be lost at one table. If you should drop that mini-bank, then pick up and leave.

Do NOT allow your playing to become a personal ego struggle with any particular dealer or casino. You must lose occasionally. Take that loss gracefully like a pro.

If you ever run into a dealer who remarks that he is "hot" (or something to that effect), or, if he says he has been beating them all day, believe him—don't play with him. Probability is a funny bird. It runs in streaks more often than not. When this happens— COOL IT. Take a walk, leave, get out, eat lunch, take a break, but stop playing.

We could devote an entire page to this next phrase; we probably should. Let it suffice just once, "When you are cold, cool off."

Ruination and Bankrolling

With an unlimited bankroll, there is no chance of ruination (losing your entire bankroll), and we could express your chances of ruination mathematically as 0%. With an extremely large bankroll and a very small maximum bet, our chances for losing the entire bankroll might be about 0.00000001% (still practically zero). The trick is to find an acceptable level of risk with a given sum of money and as large a maximum bet as is "safe."

There are three bankrolling combinations that will be described for your consideration. Each has a different ruination factor listed as a percentage. A 10% ruination means that there is a 10% chance of losing your entire bankroll. Obviously, the lower the percent ruination, the "safer" it is.

Table 8

BANKROLLING METHOD 1

5 times Maximum Bet = Mini-Bank
10 times Mini-Bank = Playing Bank (Bankroll)

5% Ruination

With a total bankroll of $2,000 each mini-bank (10%) is $200 and the maximum bet would be $40 (5 times 40=200).

Table 9

BANKROLLING METHOD 2

10 times Maximum Bet = Mini-Bank
10 times Mini-Bank = Total Playing Bank (Bankroll)

1% Ruination

Table 10
BANKROLLING METHOD 3

Maximum Bet=Total Playing Bank (Bankroll)÷100
Mini-Bank=10% of Bankroll

0.001% Ruination

Method 3 is basically the same as Method 2. The difference is that the maximum bet is *always* held to 1% of the bankroll. For example, with a $2,000 Playing Bank, the maximum bet is $20, the same as Method 2. However, if the bankroll drops to, say, $1,900, the maximum bet becomes $19.

Similarly, if the bankroll increases to $2,100, the maximum bet becomes $21. Mini-banks become 10% of the entire bankroll at the time they are used. A mini-bank from a $2,500 bankroll is $250, while later on in the playing session a mini-bank might become $300 (10% of $3,000). Because the bet size decreases if the bankroll is decreased, the ruination factor is a low 0.001%. This is the safest of the three methods.

Methods 1 and 2 are significantly more risky (a calculated risk, not a gamble) than Method 3, and they really should only be used by more aggressive players or those who wish to build up from a small bankroll as quickly as possible. Once a bankroll of one to two thousand dollars has been reached, Method 3 becomes more and more attractive.

CHAPTER 14

HOW TO USE YOUR MONEY

This chapter contains all the tips you will need to handle your bankroll. Some of these items have been stated in previous chapters and are reiterated here for the sake of convenience and emphasis. Three basic subject areas are covered. These are: BETTING, PURCHASING YOUR CHIPS, and CONCEALING YOUR WINNINGS.

Betting

In the course of this and other discussions, we will use the term "unit." This term is generally taken to mean the size of your minimum bet or, perhaps, the size of the casino chips that you are using. Thus, if you were playing with red chips, $5, your unit would be $5. Green chips are $25. Tokens are usually made of metal and have replaced the silver dollars, now out of general circulation. Your unit could be an odd number as well; possibly $2.50, $3.00, $6.00 or any basic minimum bet that you choose.

Ideally, a player would realize an enormous advantage if he were to play only when the deck becomes favorable and sit out those hands when the deck becomes poor. This practice works particularly well in the multiple-deck games which tend to hold a rich or poor pattern over a longer period of time. This practice, when used too often, will give away your style of play. One well-known system player, generally referred to as "Junior," would do just that. He bet $500 when the deck became rich. He would even try to bet $500 on someone else's hand. Junior can't play in any casino in Nevada today because he is too well known.

The next best thing to sitting out poor deck conditions is to have as wide a unit spread between the table minimum and what your bankroll will allow as a maximum. Generally, a ten unit spread is desired. For example, with a bankroll of $2,000 using Method 2, your maximum bet size would be $20. To achieve a ten unit spread, your minimum bet would have to be $2. It should be obvious that if you were playing at a $5 minimum table, your unit spread would only be four units (4 times $5 = $20). You must coordinate your bankroll with your betting so that your maximum bet is ten times the size of your minimum bet. In Atlantic City you can use a much larger bet spread.

Once you have set your maximum bet, NEVER change it during that session. To do so borders on gambling. The practice of increasing one's bet constantly, especially on a losing streak, is referred to as "steaming." Steaming is usually accompanied by increased frustration and turning red in the face. If you look around the casino, you will find some poor sap who has lost his self-control and is steaming along to certain failure. Let us repeat this point for emphasis: NEVER EXCEED YOUR MAXIMUM BET. This does not apply to splitting pairs or doubling down when you have made a maximum bet; naturally you must split and double as directed. As your bankroll grows, you will change your betting level, in accordance with the Bankrolling Methods described earlier.

Table 11

BETTING STRATEGY

DECK CONDITION	YOUR BET IS:
Poor	1 Unit
Neutral	5 Units
Rich	10 Units

Avoid entering the game in the middle of a shuffle, unless you have been counting from the beginning. When you do not know the count, wait until the deck is reshuffled. This rule is even more applicable in the multiple-deck games (see Part IV for information regarding multiple decks).

After the reshuffle, don't always make your new bet only one unit. This system gives you an advantage at the beginning of a new deck in a favorable single-deck game (Las Vegas Strip). You can afford to bet more than one unit in this case.

Don't give away your betting level by making your first bet at a new table only one unit. If you start with a big bet, your other betting patterns will confuse the dealer. Most people start out with a small bet, to get the feel of things. Because you know that you have the edge with a complete deck, make a four- to six-unit bet. It is easy to pull back your level later without raising any suspicion.

The house just loves progressive betting system players. Pretend to be one when you increase your bet. Mutter some phrase like "double-up and win" in a soft tone. This is typical behavior for the bad player, but it is something you will do when the deck changes from poor to rich. If you won a small bet when the deck was poor, then it turned rich, mutter something like "let it ride" as you restack your chips. This move is also called *parlaying a winner.* You might mention the word "parlay" as you make this increased bet.

The most powerful technique that a system player can use in the casino is referred to as "end play." Unfortunately, you will not be able to get away with it, as the casinos have been damaged effectively by this technique and are on the alert for it. If you are willing to blow a casino or a whole town, here's how it works.

Play as many hands as you can, making minimum bets. Play enough hands so that there will not be enough cards left to finish the hands without reshuffling (preferably near the very end). You can judge just how many hands you will have to play to achieve this. Naturally, there cannot be any other players at the table. Now hit all your hands that contain aces and 10's, even if you have twenty. Even hit naturals. The object is to force these cards into the discard pile so that they will be reshuffled for the next hand. The smaller and poorer cards are kept out by your standing on the hands that hold these cards. The next round of hands will be dealt from a deck that is 10- and ace-rich, so you will make maximum bets several hands during this next round. By the way, you need a much larger bankroll to use end-play.

At all times it is best to be deceptive about your incremental increases in betting. One way to do this is by not always using one chip (either $1, $5, or $25) as your minimum bet. Also, try acting a little bit. If you are not a professional, be careful not to overdo it. Show mild anger when you lose and mild delight when you win, as if to say, "How lucky I am." Be sure that you don't delude yourself into thinking that it is a matter of "luck." This might help your acting, but not your play.

Purchasing Chips

How you handle your money is a significant part of your playing style. Don't cash in immediately for an entire mini-bank at one table. Pull out a couple of rumpled bills that will cover about two maximum bets. If you have to dig into your pockets for a double down or a pair split, so much the better. This gives the impression that you are a continuous loser who can barely cover his bets.

Cashing in right away for a whole mini-bank will draw at least some attention to you. In addition, doing this removes chips from the dealer's rack and puts a big stack in front of you.

Don't carry a big wad of freshly-minted money. Such a bankroll implies that you are a winner, and it could set you up for one of the many pickpockets or muggers who frequent casinos in search of high-rollers. These may seem like small points sometimes, but they all add up when you are creating an image that you want to portray.

Concealing Winnings

This is a very important part of your playing method. Always try to give the impression of being just one of the other suckers, a loser. As mentioned before, don't place a large amount of money in front of you right away. Give the impression of continually having to dig for more money.

As you begin to win and accumulate a stack of chips, begin to remove some without any fanfare (and preferably when no one is looking), and slip them in your pocket or purse. Of course, don't be obvious about what you are doing; act nonchalantly. If you need more money, don't go for the chips; cash in some more bills.

The floorman is careful to observe the dealer's rack to see that it is full. Do not win too much from any one table, as you will be noticed. Move your action around and take a little bit from each of them. When you do stack your chips on the table, place small checks on top of big ones. If the floorman only glances in your direction, he will think that you have less. Don't stack up your checks too neatly. It makes it easier for them to count your winnings.

The Importance of Attitude

At this point, we should not have to sell you on the fact that the game of Blackjack can be beaten. The question is, "Can you do it?" Let us assure you that, if you have managed to come this far, you have the ability to do it. If the terms and expressions used here are unfamiliar to you, and the concept is new, do not be disheartened. A little time will make it all quite clear!

It has been our experience that success in any endeavor in life is more a question of attitude than anything else, surpassing knowledge, experience and money. If, on the one hand, you believe that you can succeed, you have a good chance of doing so, provided you are willing to make the necessary effort.

The principal ingredient in learning to use and profit from this system is DISCIPLINE. Your play must be disciplined, in line with the instructions presented. However, it must not appear to be disciplined to the casually observant casino personnel.

Speaking of attitude—what is the attitude of the casino? What they want is simply to relieve you of your money, smoothly and without any complaints. To do this they will distract you, wear you down, get you drunk, exert pressure on you with dirty or suspicious looks from floormen and pit bosses, or make you feel guilty for winning.

Since you are aware of what they have in mind, and you now know that you have the knowledge and ability to beat them, you should have an attitude of CONFIDENCE. You can WIN. You will win. Hold these thoughts foremost in your mind. With this attitude you are now prepared to beat them NOT at their game, but at YOUR game.

CHAPTER 15

RULES OF CASINO PLAY

There are a number of things that you should NOT do. We will list them here. They are critical to your attitude, and will indirectly affect the quality of your play in ways that you will not even be aware of consciously.

1. Do NOT drink any alcoholic beverages before or during the time that you play. If you must drink, wait until after the playing session, or before you go to sleep, so that you can sleep it off.

2. Do NOT play if you are disturbed, or there is an emotional crisis on your mind. Even the slightest upset in your emotional equilibrium will affect your play. Set your affairs at ease and aside. Otherwise, you are like the proverbial incompetent executive who continually brings his home troubles with him to the office. If you are overly troubled, don't play—do something else. Playing this system requires your total mental capacity.

3. Before you begin to play for large stakes, be sure that you are "UP." Practice with smaller stakes, but follow all the principles outlined, especially those related to regular movement from table to table. DON'T kid yourself into thinking that the casino is not concerned about a winning dollar bettor—they are. If you are tired, DON'T play. If you cannot concentrate, DON'T play. If anything at all bothers you, DON'T play.

4. Your ability to continuously use this system is dependent upon your anonymity and the casino's inability to recognize you and other players who use this system. To this effect, you must NEVER brag about your accomplishments. Satisfy your ego by chuckling ALL THE WAY TO THE BANK. It is none of your friends', relatives', or anybody else's business where you earn your money. What you are doing is perfectly legal, but you must remain incognito. A casual acquaintance, especially in Nevada, could be a casino employee. Your interest is the opposite to his. He needs the casinos to take your money so they can pay his wages. You want to take that money from them. He or she will report you.

5. We are repeating this next point because it is important, NEVER play with SCARED money. If you can't afford to lose your total playing bank, then don't play with it. It will have an effect on your mental state.

6. Do not ANTAGONIZE the dealer. You will lose and you will have bad streaks, just as you will have good streaks. Do not take your frustrations out on the dealer. Be friendly, smile—but DON'T engage in excessive conversation to the point where the dealer will recognize you readily. If you sense that the dealer wants to see you lose, get up and play somewhere else. He could be cheating you.

7. DON'T do anything that will cause the house to suspect you of being a cheat. Your appearance should be neat. If appropriate, wear short sleeves. See that your hands and nails are relatively clean so that it doesn't look like you are marking the cards. Keep your actions down to a minimum. Do NOT handle the cards excessively. Do NOT make fast moves with the cards. Avoid any unique hand, arm, body, or head movements that might be characteristic of you as an individual, and could serve as a basis for future recognition. Ask your spouse or a trusted associate to observe you while you play so that they can point out mannerisms of yours which might clearly identify you.

8. Do NOT forget to keep records of your activities, as explained in a previous section. Use the format presented, or make up your own. Do NOT let anyone see you using this form. Wait until you leave the casino, or go to the rest room to do your accounting. Keep your playing orderly, in the way you have planned. Remember that each casino is in reality three casinos, as there are three shifts of workers. If you are to play twice at the same casino, try to mix up your playing time so you play different shifts to reduce your visibility.

9. Do NOT play in the casino just after the main show gets out. This is when it is most crowded. You will only be able to put in a limited day's effort at any rate, so pick the hours that are most profitable. You will personally have to check this out, since it varies with the time of the year and day of the week.

The Casino's Attitude

We will now discuss the attitude of the casino toward players. Perhaps the best analogy one can make is to compare the players to sheep and the casino to a shepherd. After they've fed you, have seen that you're comfortable, have allowed you to romp merrily in the fields, they gently take the wool (shirt) off your back. However, they don't wish to damage your hide so that you can grow another coat (let you go home and earn some more money), so they put you out to pasture until the next shearing session.

In plainer language, the object of the casinos is to take your money, as much as they can get, and make you like it—or at least not feel too bad. When given the choice of making you feel bad or taking your money, you can be sure they will choose the latter.

The casino regards players as SUCKERS. They are treated as such by feeding them free drinks, breaking their concentration with the noise of glaring bands and piped music, as well as playing upon their most basic and vulnerable emotion, sex. Scantily-clad waitresses and showgirls for the men and distinguished-looking floormen for the ladies are part of casino fare.

When a player starts to win conspicuously, they will attempt to feed him more drinks, talk to him, and otherwise confuse him into making stupid plays. They may cast suspicious eyes, whisper behind his back, and generally give him HEAT to try to unbalance him on the one hand, and make him feel guilty for winning on the other.

When the casino spots a consistent winner they will take many countermeasures against him, as explained in another section. The ultimate countermeasure is being BARRED from playing Blackjack in that casino. You see, the casinos are in business to make money. They don't want WINNERS in their place; only losers are welcome to play.

CHAPTER 16

ANALYZING THE CASINO

It would not be possible for us to give you an acccurate analysis of where to play because the rules are constantly being changed (the casino lists are intended as a *guide,* though they were carefully researched and should be fairly reliable). At the moment, due to its more liberal rules, Las Vegas is favored, in general, over Tahoe, Reno, and Atlantic City, in that order. We have, instead, presented a format for you to use in making your own analysis when you arrive at the general area where you will be playing.

Take a piece of ruled paper (you may need more than one sheet), and place the headings down the side, as indicated in Chart H. Chart H is used as follows. On the left side are the rules or other conditions that will affect your overall percentage, followed by a number which is weighed in accordance with the extent that that rule or condition does affect your percentage. After checking out a casino, write the name of the casino on top and put in all the numbers that apply to that casino. The total is used to compare one casino with another; the higher the total, the better for the player. A Las Vegas Strip single-deck game, no Surrender or DASA, with a thirty-nine card shuffle point would have a total of 466. A Reno single-deck game with a thirty-nine card shuffle point would have a total of 391. In general, try to play in a casino with a rating of at least 300.

CHART H

ANALYZING THE CASINO

	Rule or Condition	Points	Name of Casino								
	Insurance	+ 210									
	Pair Splitting Allowed	+ 46									
	Resplitting Of Pairs Except Aces	+ 10									
	Resplitting Allowed On Aces	+ 10									
Doubling Down Allowed On	11	+ 89									
	10	+ 56									
	9	+ 14									
	8	+ 1									
	SOFT	+ 40									
	Late Surrender	+ 20									
	Early Surrender	+ 65									
	Doubling Allowed On Three Or More Cards	+ 20									
	DASA	+ 20									
Shuffle Point	If Less Than 1/2	Do Not Play									
	1/2	− 100									
	2/3	− 25									
	3/4	± 0									
	7/8	+ 25									
	All	+ 100									
Number Of Decks	1	0									
	2	− 35									
	4	− 51									
	5	− 54									
	6	− 56									
	More Than 6	− 65									
	Dealer Hits Soft 17	− 20									
	Blackjack Pays Even Money	− 206									
	Blackjack Pays Double	+ 206									
	TOTAL										
	Number Of Tables										

PART IV

MULTI-DECK PLAY
AND
TIPS FROM A PROFESSIONAL PLAYER

CHAPTER 17

MULTIPLE-DECK PLAY

Over the past decade and especially in the last few years, the trend has been toward fewer single-deck games and more two-, four-, five-, six-, and even eight-deck games. There are several reasons the casinos have increased the number of multi-deck games.

In single-deck Blackjack, the dealer must shuffle every few hands if the table is full. This takes up time that could be profitably used for taking money from all the unskilled players. With multiple decks there is less shuffling, thus less wasted time. In addition, multiple-deck games can be dealt more quickly from a shoe (the rack that feeds the cards to the dealer), thus saving even more time.

There is less likely to be any cheating in multiple-deck games. A few marked cards in a single deck will make quite a difference; whereas, the effect is severely lessened as the number of decks is increased. Many of the games are dealt face up; the player never touches the cards, just signals his playing decisions by hand. Multiple decks also make it much more difficult for the dealer to deal "seconds," or to work in concert with a player against the house. The State of Nevada has granted some casinos licenses for multiple-deck play only, or for shoes used to hold cards (usually small casinos with four tables or less). The Gaming Control Board does not have enough personnel to properly regulate all the 200+ unrestricted (table games) licensees in the State. Shoes tend to limit cheating, and so the Board assumes this will hold down its enforcement problems. The failure to increase personnel in this field is additional proof of the irresponsible and indefensible position of the State when it comes to protecting the public. Lastly, most casino personnel believe that it is virtually impossible for anyone to consistently win at multiple-deck games. Fortunately, they are quite mistaken. But it works to the system player's advantage for the casinos to think that they are completely safe from counters.

It is true that a four-deck game is less favorable to the Basic Strategy player. Basic Strategy in a single-deck game virtually nullifies the house advantage. In a four-deck game, however, the Basic Strategy player has a disadvantage of about 0.5%.

Multiple deck is also less advantageous in that it requires a more sustained sense of concentration. It is therefore much easier for fatigue to take its toll and reduce accuracy.

With practice and diligence, however, these factors can be overcome so that multiple-deck play in Las Vegas, Reno, Atlantic City, and other casino areas throughout the world will become quite profitable indeed.

Adjustments for Multiple-Deck Play

Only learn those charts for counting that are applicable to the area you are going to play. As you go to a different area, you can learn the appropriate chart.

Chart 7-1 contains the appropriate count tables for Ace Count for one, two, four, six, and eight decks. Various adjustments need to be made from a normal mathematical relationship that has already been compensated for in the charts. There is no need for you to do anything but memorize the chart you are going to use.

A similar statement can be made for Chart 7-2, Five Count for one, two, four, six, and eight decks.

Chart 7-3 makes an adjustment for four groups of decks remaining to be played: one and two, three and four, five and six, and seven and eight.

Chart 7–4 makes an adjustment that is not easily recognized, except when you realize that the poor condition (zero) is constant.

Betting Spreads

You can increase your betting spread by a larger amount in a multiple-deck game. This does not have to be done in one fell swoop. The deck has a tendency to hold a rich or poor condition longer in a multiple-deck game so you can increase to say ten units when the deck becomes rich, then jump to 20 when it stays there or go to 40 if it continues to stay rich. Do not forget that you must be bankrolled for the maximum bet.

Strategy

The appropriate changes for different playing conditions you will commonly find (numbers of decks, rule changes, etc.), are covered in the Appendix—Basic Strategy Tables. Be sure to use the correct Basic Strategy for the game conditions that you are to play under. The wrong strategy will result in a lower return or possible losses.

CHAPTER 18

TIPS FROM A PROFESSIONAL

1. FOLLOW ALL OF THE "CASINO PLAY RULES" TO THE LETTER AND ALL BANKROLLING RULES.
2. NEVER LOSE MORE THAN ONE MINI-BANK AT ANY ONE TABLE. Be sure to get the dealer's name and description. If you have lost two mini-banks to any one dealer without having offsetting wins, NEVER PLAY WITH THAT DEALER AGAIN!
3. NEVER LOSE MORE THAN TWO MINI-BANKS IN ANY ONE DAY. This is a protective measure for the player against getting mentally upset. You must have a positive attitude at all times while playing.
4. NEVER STAY OVER 45 MINUTES IN ANY ONE CASINO. This will be one of the hardest rules for a beginning player to follow, but a player must heed this in order to protect his anonymity.
5. ALWAYS TRY TO PLAY WITH YOUNG, FRIENDLY, FEMALE DEALERS. It takes time to develop the skills needed to become a mechanic. A friendly dealer will take less notice of your bet variations.
6. BETTING:
   a. *Single Deck.* Occasionally you will have a maximum bet up and the dealer will reshuffle the deck. Do not pull back on the size of that bet. Let it ride; you still have an advantage off the top of a fresh deck. If you are playing against rules less advantageous than on the Las Vegas Strip, break your bet into two bets of five units each. Another trick to use

is to keep your chips in a pile (not stacked up); when the dealer is shuffling, stack your chips, including your bet, like you're counting your money, and then come out with a one- or two-unit bet. With a little time and practice you will be able to anticipate when a dealer is going to shuffle. If a dealer is varying the point of the shuffle, leave the table. He may be counting. The third time a dealer shuffles just after you place your bet (MAXIMUM) leave the table and find a dealer who does not reshuffle when you place your maximum bet.

b. *Double Deck.* Always pull down your maximum bet if the dealer reshuffles; to do otherwise in the 50–50 position off the top of a double-deck game would be bordering on "gambling." Always make a one-unit bet at the start.

c. *Shoe Games.* NEVER start off a shoe game in the middle of a round.

d. *Other.* If you wish to play all positions (RICH to POOR) in a multiple-deck game, you must increase your unit spread in accordance with the number of decks you are playing against. For example, if you played all deck conditions in a four-deck game, your minimum (POOR) bet would remain at one unit, but your mid bet (NEUTRAL) would now be 20 units and your maximum (RICH) bet would be 40 units. This is acceptable, but would require a much larger TOTAL PLAYING BANK.

7. NEVER LEAVE THE TABLE ABRUPTLY. Ease yourself out of your seat and walk away. Do not look back. The pit boss' and the dealer's eyes may be following you. Don't act as if anything out of the ordinary is occurring. They may think that you are a system player, but they will never **REALLY** know.

8. TOKES. It is not necessary to toke the dealer—to give him/her a tip. If you do this, use it to your advantage. Never give the dealer money outright. Always make a bet for him. Dealers will not usually break the deck down when you have

a bet up for them. So make the bet for him when the deck is rich and you wish it kept in play. It is generally a good policy to keep the dealers happy. If you are winning large sums, a little oil on the water may keep things going well for you. If you do particularly well, it is bad practice not to give something to the dealer—they may remember you unfavorably the next time, but be sure to put the amount you toked under the "TOKE" column on your Casino Activity Log (Chart G). Remember that the chips you give away should be recorded under the "WIN" column of your Casino Activity Log.

9. SCHEDULE YOUR PLAY. When scheduling, keep in mind the rules in each casino and the length of your stay. If you are in a gaming town for only three or four days, you should NEVER play in the same casino on the same shift more than once.

10. PLAYING POSITION. Always seek a head-up game with the dealer. When you are playing alone with the dealer you can naturally see all the cards except for the dealer's hole card. Avoid sitting in third base. Sit in the middle of the table. From this position you will have a better chance to see the other players' cards. Try to see them all before you have to make any playing decisions. This will allow you to get the greatest amount of information regarding the probability of what is coming off the top of the deck and what the dealer has in the hole. Also, by sitting in the middle you can—by body language—keep other players away by taking up a lot of room.

11. APPEARANCE. Without being obvious, give the appearance of being stupid and ignorant. If you can do it well, ask the dealer for help occasionally; act as if you can't add up your hand. This may be easy to do when you have a soft hand with three or more cards. Say something like, "What have I got here?" while showing him your hand. In other words, don't act like you are a GOOD player and know all

about the game. Appear to be a little tipsy; this is normal for the typical player. Appear interested in things other than the game. The attractive waitresses (if you're a man) or the handsome floormen (if you're a woman) might be subjects for complimentary comments or questions. Distract the dealer from noticing your ability as a player with small talk about the weather, the music, anything insignificant. Don't watch the cards too closely. Be casual about how you observe, but be sure to take everything in. This is a particularly difficult move, but you will soon master it. You might want to prolong your anonymity by using disguises. This will work, provided you follow certain principles. NEVER use a disguise that is obviously a disguise. This will attract more attention than it is worth. Avoid going into the casino as your real self if you are going to use disguises. In this manner, they will not have the base from which to recognize you. Switch your appearances around frequently so that none of your images become too fixed in the eyes of the casino personnel. Disguises can be fun— and there are many easy ways to disguise yourself—unless you are that one distinctive type of person who either by size, shape, color, deformity or other obvious physical trait, would be wasting his/her time trying to alter your appearance. There are a number of articles suitable for disguise. These include: wigs, moustaches, jewelry, clothing, eye glasses, contacts, color-change contact lenses, etc. Be careful not to spend the money for a disguise and then wear something distinctive, like a ring or watch or article of clothing, which will be the undoing of that disguise. With wigs for both men and women being acceptable wear, a disguise can be quite easy to come by and effective to use. Be careful how you dress. You don't want to stand out or be noticed, so dress like the majority of the people who are in the casino where you're playing.

12. GENERAL ADVICE. Play with as few people as possible. The number of other people and how they play will have NO effect on the percentage you will win. But the fewer number of other players, the more hands you will get per hour. The easiest way to increase your percentage is to increase your unit spread; for example, play one to 20 on a single deck instead of one to five or ten. The fewer number of decks used, the higher your percentage. The more player options available, the higher your percentage. The further into the deck or decks that the dealers deal, the higher your winning percentage will be.

> **NOW THAT YOU HAVE READ THE ENTIRE TEXT, PLEASE READ IT AGAIN.**

After you have done this, proceed to the "HOW TO STUDY" section. If you should have trouble in that section, please see the learning assistance options listed in the beginning of this book.

HOW TO STUDY

This step-by-step learning method MUST be followed EXACTLY if you are to gain the full benefits of this system.

You will need the following materials before proceeding:

1. Eight NEW decks of cards (do not use plastic-coated cards).
2. Detach the Basic Strategy Tables (in the Appendix) at the back of the book and save them until you are instructed to use them.
3. Detach the Flash Card pages at the back of the book, but do not cut them up into individual cards until you're ready to begin Lesson 1.

The lesson sequence is as follows:

Lesson 1 (Basic Strategy)

Lesson 2 (Ace Count) plus Lesson 1 (Basic Strategy)

Lesson 3 (Five Count) plus Lesson 1 (Basic Strategy)

Lesson 4 (Combination Ace-Five Count) plus Lesson 1 (Basic Strategy)

Lesson 5 (HI-OPT Count) plus Lesson 1 (Basic Strategy)

Lesson 6 (Simulated Casino Play)

Lesson 7 (Casino Play—Single Deck)

Lesson 8 (Multi-Deck Play)

Lesson 9 (Casino Play—Multi-Deck)

Lesson 1 (Basic Strategy) is used with each subsequent lesson through Lesson 5. Lessons 2 through 5 get progressively more difficult and should be studied in the order that they are given. DO NOT go to Lesson 6 (or beyond) until you are instructed.

LESSON 1 (BASIC STRATEGY)

STEP A—Use Basic Strategy Flash Cards to familiarize yourself with the rules. (Flash Cards B-1 through B-30.)

STEP B—Open one deck of cards, shuffle, and play Basic Strategy. Play the dealer's hand, but do not use any chips. Whenever you deal to yourself, keep your hand in front of you and the dealer's hand away from you. This is the way that you will see the cards in the casino, so study them in this manner. When you feel comfortable using Basic Strategy (do not memorize it, but practice until it comes naturally), go to STEP C.

STEP C—Take the quiz at the back of the book. Complete the Single Deck section only. If you do not score 100%, go back to Step A.

NOTE: Basic Strategy is used with ALL four Intermediate Level Counting Systems. It must be practiced and practiced until it becomes an almost automatic response for you. When you reach that point, go directly to Lesson 2.

LESSON 2 (ACE COUNT)

STEP A—Using one deck, make four 13-card stacks; then make two 26-card stacks; then one 13-card stack and one 39-card stack. Repeat this step, randomly stacking cards and then guessing the number of quarter decks in each stack until you reach an accuracy level of calling the quarter decks correctly nine out of ten times. Do not go to STEP B until you have mastered this step.

STEP B—Memorize Chart 7-1 for single deck. When you have done so, go to STEP C.

STEP C—Using one deck, turn over one card at a time counting +1 for each ace you see. At each count, check the number of quarter decks played and note condition of the deck. Do this step several times correctly before going to STEP D.

STEP D—Using a single deck, play Basic Strategy. Remember, deal your hand in front of you and the dealer's hand away from you. While playing, keep a running ace count (+1). After each ace count determine the condition of the deck. Stop periodically after an ace count to check on the accuracy of your quarter-deck count. Do this step until Basic Strategy and the Ace Count become an almost automatic response. When that happens, go to Lesson 6.

LESSON 3 (FIVE COUNT)

STEP A—Memorize Chart 7-2 for single deck. When you have done this, go to STEP B.

STEP B—Using one deck, turn over one card at a time counting +1 for each five you see. At each count, check quarter decks played and note condition of the deck. Do this step several times before going to STEP C.

STEP C—Using a single deck, play Basic Strategy. Remember, deal your hand in front of you and the dealer's hand away from you. While playing, keep a running five count (+1). After each five count determine the condition of the deck. Stop periodically after a five count to check on the accuracy of your quarter-deck count. Do this step until Basic Strategy and the Five Count become an almost automatic response. When that happens go to Lesson 6.

LESSON 4 (COMBINATION ACE-FIVE COUNT)

STEP A—Memorize Chart 7–3 for single deck. When you have done this, go to STEP B.

STEP B—Using one deck, turn over one card at a time counting +1 for each ace you see and -1 for each 5. At each count, check quarter decks played and note condition of the deck. Do this step several times before going to STEP C.

STEP C—Using a single deck, play Basic Strategy. Remember, deal your hand in front of you and the dealer's hand away from you. While playing, keep a running ace count (+1) as well as a running five count (−1). Remember, you need only keep the SUM of these numbers in your head. So, if you see one ace and one five, the SUM would be zero.

It is important to practice this step until you can go back and forth across the zero point without making any errors. When you have mastered these three steps, go to Lesson 6.

LESSON 5 (HI-OPT COUNT)

STEP A—Memorize Chart 7–4 for single deck. When you have done this, go to STEP B.

STEP B—Using one deck, turn over one card at a time counting +1 for each 3, 4, 5, and 6 you see and −1 for each ten, Jack, Queen, or King you see. (Keep in mind that all other cards have a value of zero and therefore are not counted.) This step will take extensive practice before it is mastered. As you keep a running count of the +1 and −1 cards also note the condition of the deck. When this step has been mastered, go to STEP C.

STEP C—Using a single deck, play Basic Strategy. Remember, deal your hand in front of you and the dealer's hand away from you. While playing, keep a running count of all the +1 and −1 cards. Stop periodically to check on the accuracy of your quarter-deck count. Do this step until you feel confident that you are combining Basic Strategy and the HI-OPT Count, keeping errors to a minimum. When that happens, go to Lesson 6.

LESSON 6 (SIMULATED CASINO PLAY)

STEP A—Go through the flash cards for Basic Strategy twice, repeating any missed cards ten times. Repeat this step twice.

STEP B—Deal out the cards (two for you and one for the dealer), and say the rule or rules that apply. Go through one deck twice.

STEP C—Have someone deal to you (or deal to yourself if you can't find another person). Use one of the Intermediate Level Count Systems, Basic Strategy, and chips so that this practice more closely resembles actual casino play. Handle your betting in accordance with the section on betting in Part III of this text.

STEP D—Practice dealing, counting, and betting. Run through deck at least five times, varying the number of hands in each game. Do this step until you feel confident that you have mastered Basic Strategy, an Intermediate count system, and the proper betting strategy. When that happens, go to Lesson 7.

LESSON 7 (CASINO PLAY—SINGLE DECK)

STEP A—You should now be ready to begin playing in the casinos. Before you start playing, however, we strongly urge you to stop in at one of our schools so you can completely check out your newly acquired skills. There will be a small charge for this service, but it could save you thousands of dollars at the tables. (If you are a former student, there is no charge for this service should you return to the original school you attended.)

STEP B—Play for three hours in the casinos, making only flat bets of one or two dollars (whatever the table minimum is). Do not bet more than five dollars.

STEP C—Play twenty hours (table time) in the casinos using proper "bankrolling," following all the "Casino Play Rules" and the "Tips From a Professional" that apply to single deck. DO NOT play any multi-decks (obviously not possible in Atlantic City) at this time. Follow the Betting Strategy listed in Table 11.

STEP D—Keep a record of your play in half-hour segments on your Casino Activity Log.

LESSON 8 (SIMULATED MULTI-DECK PLAY)

STEP A—Study multi-deck play described in Part IV.

STEP B—Cut out remaining flash cards, add them to Basic Strategy cards, and learn all the rules including those for multi-deck play.

STEP C—Practice dealing and counting (using one of the four count systems). Run through shoe at least three times, varying the number of hands in each game.

STEP D—Learn the rules appropriate for the area you will be playing in and follow the procedures in the previous lessons as if starting over with your new set of rules.

STEP E—Take the quiz at the back of the book for multiple deck in your area of play. If you do not score 100% you are not ready. Review all of the previous steps.

STEP F—Deal the appropriate multi-deck game to yourself and follow all the rules that apply to multi-deck games. Play Basic Strategy and one of the four count systems. Use chips to more closely simulate casino playing.

STEP G—When you can get the card count and the deck count correct nine out of ten times with the multi-deck shoe, go to Lesson 9.

LESSON 9 (CASINO PLAY—MULTI-DECK)

STEP A—You are now ready to begin playing in the casinos. Here again, before you start playing, however, we strongly urge you to stop in at one of our schools so you can completely check out your newly acquired skills. See **STEP A** in **LESSON 7**.

STEP B—Play for three hours in the casinos, making only flat bets of one or two dollars (whatever the table minimum is). Do not bet more than five dollars.

STEP C—Play twenty hours (table time) in the casinos using proper "bankrolling," following all the "Casino Play Rules" and the "Tips From a Professional" that apply to multi-deck play. Follow the Betting Strategy listed in Table 11.

•••

Congratulations! You should now be ready to play "WINNING BLACKJACK" throughout the world. If you have any trouble, we again suggest that you call our school office and let us show you how we can help.

•••

QUIZ

1. An example of a soft hand is: _____
   a. An ace and a 4.
   b. An ace and two 3's.
   c. Two aces.
   d. An ace, a 2 and a 3.
   e. All of the above.

2. One difference between playing on the Strip in Las Vegas and playing downtown in Las Vegas is that at the downtown casinos:

_____
   a. You are not allowed to double after the split.
   b. The player is allowed to soft double.
   c. The player cannot surrender.
   d. The dealer wins all pushes.
   e. The dealer hits soft seventeen.

3. As of January 1983, the only Strip casino that allowed the player to surrender and double after the split, where dealers did not hit soft seventeen, was: _____
   a. The Riviera.
   b. Caesars Palace.
   c. The Stardust.
   d. The Silver Slipper.
   e. None of the above.

4. Casino Blackjack can be beaten because: _____
   a. It is based on independent trials.
   b. The casino does not play its hand correctly.
   c. It is based on dependent trials.
   d. Basic Strategy gives the player a 1.5% advantage.
   e. The player can double up after a loss.

5. Once you enter a casino to play Blackjack: _____
   a. You should look at every table.
   b. You should exit no later than thirty minutes later.
   c. You should ask the other players how the dealer is doing.
   d. Look for crowded tables.
   e. Do none of the above.

6. When a player splits aces, most casinos allow him: _____
   a. To surrender his hands if he doesn't like the total.
   b. To take only one card on each ace.
   c. To take as many cards on each ace as the player requests.
   d. To insure both hands against the dealer, if the dealer shows an ace.
   e. None of the above.

7. The dealer must take a card when: _____
   a. His total is seventeen or more.
   b. His total is seventeen or less.
   c. His total is sixteen or less.
   d. Any time he wants.
   e. If there is a push.

8. When the dealer's up-card is an ace, insurance is offered. This means: _____
   a. The count determines whether the player takes insurance.
   b. Insurance pays 2-to-1.
   c. The player puts up half of the amount of his original bet.
   d. If the dealer shows a ten value card in the hole, the hand is over.
   e. All of these.

9. When playing Basic Strategy, the player could double down a hard eight (5,3; 4,4) when: _____
   a. The dealer shows a 5 only.
   b. The dealer shows 4 or 5.
   c. The dealer shows 5 or 6.
   d. The dealer shows a 6 only.
   e. The dealer shows 4, 5, or 6.

10. In Las Vegas, the player may double down: _____
   a. Any two cards.
   b. Only if doubling after the split is allowed.
   c. On any three cards.
   d. Only on 8, 9, 10, 11.
   e. Any of the above times.

11. We will surrender: _____
   a. When we feel unlucky.
   b. When the dealer has won at least two hands in a row.
   c. In hands where statistics show we will lose at least 51% of the time.
   d. In hands where statistics show we will lose more than 75% of the time.
   e. At none of these times.

12. When playing Basic Strategy in a single-deck game we would split 4's: _____
   a. Against a 3.
   b. Against 4, 5, or 6 if the casino allows doubling after the split.
   c. At none of these times.

13. If the dealer shows a 9, we would stand on:_____
   a. A soft eighteen.
   b. A soft seventeen.
   c. A soft nineteen.
   d. A pair of aces.

14. Most counters do not earn the money they should because:

_____
   a. They are not properly bankrolled.
   b. They miss the count too often.
   c. They do not know the strategy or use it accurately.
   d. All of the above.
   e. None of the above.

15. Your maximum bet will be put up when:_____
   a. The deck is rich.
   b. Off the top of the deck.
   c. After you have received a Blackjack.
   d. None of the above.

16. The player is betting $20.00 and takes Insurance against the dealer's ace. The dealer does not have the 10 in the hole, so the player hard doubles his eleven. The player wins his double down. The entire transaction netted the player: _____
   a. $20.00.
   b. $10.00.
   c. $40.00.
   d. $30.00.
   e. None of the above.

17. The player's maximum bet should be: _____
   a. 1/2% of his total playing bank (TPB).
   b. 1% of his TPB.
   c. 2% of his TPB.
   d. 50% of his TPB.
   e. 10% of his TPB.

18. When using the Ace Count Single Deck, the deck is rich when: _____
   a. The count is 2 and a quarter deck has been played.
   b. The count is 4 and three quarter decks have been played.
   c. The count is 1 and two quarter decks have been played.
   d. The count is 3 and two quarter decks have been played.

19. When using the Five Count Double Deck, the deck is rich when: _____
   a. The count is 3 and two quarter decks have been played.
   b. The count is 8 and seven quarter decks have been played.
   c. The count is 5 and four quarter decks have been played.
   d. None of the above.

20. When using the Combination Ace-Five Count, 1 to 8 decks, the deck is poor when: _____
   a. The count is -4 and seven decks remain to be played.
   b. The count is -1 and three decks remain to be played.
   c. The count is -3 and two decks remain to be played.
   d. All of the above.

21. When using the HI-OPT Count, 1 to 8 decks, the deck becomes rich when: _____
   a. The count is 6 and three decks remain to be played.
   b. The count is 3 and one deck remains to be played.
   c. The count is 7 and six decks remain to be played.

22. When using the HI-OPT Count, 1 to 8 decks, Insurance should be taken when: _____
   a. The count is +9 and four decks remain to be played.
   b. The count is +12 and four decks remain to be played.
   c. The count is +21 and eight decks remain to be played.

23. If you want to tip the dealer you can: _____
   a. Actually give the money directly to the dealer.
   b. Give the money to the pit boss for the dealer.
   c. Put a chip in front of the betting box.
   d. Do any of the above.

24. At most Blackjack tables in Nevada there are:
   a. Five.
   b. Six.
   c. Seven.
   d. Eight.
   e. None of these...spots for playing a hand.

25. It is best to: _____
   a. Drink before you play.
   b. Warm up two hours before you play.
   c. Play four hours before taking a break.
   d. Play always at crowded tables.
   e. Do none of the above.

26. When a counter is attempting casino play for the very first time he should: _____
   a. Spread his units from one to two to four.
   b. Spread his units from one to six.
   c. Spread his units from one to five to ten.
   d. Flat bet.
   e. Do none of the above.

27. The very first thing the player does after his hand has been dealt is: _____
   a. Ask himself, "Do I have a Surrender hand?"
   b. Update the count.
   c. Ask himself, "Does the dealer show an ace or 10?"
   d. Take Insurance.
   e. Do none of the above.

28. The player's mini-bank should always be: _____
   a. 10%.
   b. 1%.
   c. 20%.
   d. 8%.
   e. 5%...of the player's total bank.

••

For the following questions, answer them with the corresponding rules or conditions for single deck, double deck, and four decks. You are playing in a casino on the Las Vegas Strip that allows late surrender and doubling after the split, and the dealer stands on all 17's. Blackjack pays 3-to-2, insurance is allowed and pays 2-to-1.

Answer all questions with HIT, STAND, SPLIT, DOUBLE, SURRENDER, or INSURANCE. *Do Not Give The Whole Rule.*

	Your Hand	Dealer Shows	Other Conditions	Basic Single Deck	Double Deck	Four Decks
29.	(A,4,7,2)	10	*	_____	_____	_____
30.	(8,8)	8		_____	_____	_____
31.	(A,7)	6		_____	_____	_____
32.	(9,7)	10		_____	_____	_____
33.	(9,3,4)	10	*	_____	_____	_____
34.	(7,4)	9		_____	_____	_____
35.	(10,10)	3		_____	_____	_____
36.	(10,6)	Ace	*	_____	_____	_____
37.	(6,4)	7		_____	_____	_____
38.	(7,7)	8		_____	_____	_____
39.	(10,3)	3		_____	_____	_____
40.	(9,6)	9		_____	_____	_____
41.	(6,2)	6		_____	_____	_____
42.	(A,6)	2		_____	_____	_____
43.	(10,5)	10	*	_____	_____	_____
44.	(9,4)	2		_____	_____	_____
45.	(6,4)	6		_____	_____	_____
46.	(3,3)	5		_____	_____	_____
47.	(A,4)	4		_____	_____	_____
48.	(A,7)	9		_____	_____	_____
49.	(9,9)	7		_____	_____	_____
50.	(6,A,5,4,)	10	*	_____	_____	_____
51.	(9,3)	3		_____	_____	_____
52.	(2,2)	8		_____	_____	_____
53.	(A,3,5,)	10	*	_____	_____	_____
54.	(A,A)	9		_____	_____	_____
55.	(A,4)	2		_____	_____	_____
56.	(6,3,6)	10	*	_____	_____	_____
57.	(A,7)	Ace	*	_____	_____	_____
58.	(7,4)	7		_____	_____	_____
59.	(6,6)	3		_____	_____	_____
60.	(10,10)	6		_____	_____	_____

* No Dealer BJ

	Your Hand	Dealer Shows	Other Conditions	Basic Single Deck	Double Deck	Four Decks
61.	(5,4)	8		_____	_____	_____
62.	(A,A)	6		_____	_____	_____
63.	(A,9)	6		_____	_____	_____
64.	(9,9)	9		_____	_____	_____
65.	(A,7)	2		_____	_____	_____
66.	(10,10)	6		_____	_____	_____
67.	(A,3)	3		_____	_____	_____
68.	(2,2)	5		_____	_____	_____
69.	(10,5)	Ace	*	_____	_____	_____
70.	(5,3)	5		_____	_____	_____
71.	(7,5,3)	8		_____	_____	_____
72.	(A,2)	4		_____	_____	_____
73.	(4,4)	4		_____	_____	_____
74.	(7,7)	10	*	_____	_____	_____
75.	(A,3,4)	6		_____	_____	_____

* No Dealer BJ

QUIZ ANSWERS

1.	E	8.	E	15.	A	22.	B
2.	E	9.	C	16.	D	23.	D
3.	B	10.	A	17.	B	24.	C
4.	C	11.	D	18.	C	25.	E
5.	A,B,C	12.	B	19.	A,C	26.	D
6.	B	13.	C	20.	A	27.	B
7.	C	14.	D	21.	C	28.	A

29.	HIT	HIT	HIT
30.	SPLIT	SPLIT	SPLIT
31.	DOUBLE	DOUBLE	DOUBLE
32.	SURRENDER	SURRENDER	SURRENDER
33.	HIT	HIT	HIT
34.	DOUBLE	DOUBLE	DOUBLE
35.	STAND	STAND	STAND
36.	SURRENDER	SURRENDER	SURRENDER
37.	DOUBLE	DOUBLE	DOUBLE
38.	SPLIT	HIT	HIT
39.	STAND	STAND	STAND
40.	HIT	HIT	HIT
41.	HIT	HIT	HIT
42.	DOUBLE	HIT	HIT
43.	SURRENDER	SURRENDER	SURRENDER
44.	STAND	STAND	STAND
45.	DOUBLE	DOUBLE	DOUBLE
46.	SPLIT	SPLIT	SPLIT
47.	DOUBLE	DOUBLE	DOUBLE
48.	HIT	HIT	HIT

49.	STAND	STAND	STAND
50.	HIT	HIT	HIT
51.	HIT	HIT	HIT
52.	HIT	HIT	HIT
53.	STAND	STAND	STAND
54.	SPLIT	SPLIT	SPLIT
55.	HIT	HIT	HIT
56.	HIT	HIT	HIT
57.	STAND	STAND	STAND
58.	DOUBLE	DOUBLE	DOUBLE
59.	SPLIT	SPLIT	SPLIT
60.	STAND	STAND	STAND
61.	HIT	HIT	HIT
62.	SPLIT	SPLIT	SPLIT
63.	STAND	STAND	STAND
64.	SPLIT	SPLIT	SPLIT
65.	STAND	STAND	STAND
66.	STAND	STAND	STAND
67.	HIT	HIT	HIT
68.	SPLIT	SPLIT	SPLIT
69.	HIT	HIT	HIT
70.	DOUBLE	DOUBLE	DOUBLE
71.	HIT	HIT	HIT
72.	DOUBLE	HIT	HIT
73.	SPLIT	HIT	HIT
74.	SURRENDER	HIT	HIT
75.	STAND	STAND	STAND

APPENDIX

FLASH CARDS

The flash cards that appear on the following pages should be cut along the dotted line and used as study aids. The cards are designed to be held in the left hand, with the thumb covering the answer. Read the card, recite the answer, and slide the card out with your right hand. Your left thumb will conceal the answer on the next card.

Each card is keyed to identify the set to which it belongs:

B = Basic Strategy
D = Double Deck
BAC = Basic Strategy, Atlantic City
MB = Basic Strategy, Multiple Deck

BASIC SINGLE DECK (LAS VEGAS):

B1—B30

BASIC SINGLE DECK (RENO):

Note: DASA not allowed.
Dealer Hits Soft 17.

B3—B12, B21—B29

BASIC DOUBLE DECK:

Note: Remove D1, D2,
if Surrender does not apply.

D1—D14, B4, B6, B9—B12,
B14—B16, B18, B20, B21,
B23, B24, B26—B28.

BASIC FOUR DECK:

Note: Remove D1, D2, MB1,
if Surrender does not apply.

D1—D10, D13, D14,
MB1—MB3, B4, B6,
B9—B12, B14, B16, B18,
B21, B23, B24, B26—B28.

BASIC ATLANTIC CITY:

Note: DASA applies.

D3—D10, D13, D14,
MB1—MB3, B4, B6, B9—B12,
B14, B16, B18, B21, B23, B24,
B26—B28, Add in BAC1, BAC2.

(If Early Surrender applies; otherwise remove all Surrender
Flash cards—MB1, BAC1, BAC2.)

SURRENDER STRATEGY	SURRENDER STRATEGY
DEALER SHOWS	DEALER SHOWS
ACE	**10**
	SURRENDER (10,6) (10,5) (9,7) (9,6)
SURRENDER 10,6 B1	or (7,7) B2

PAIR SPLITTING STRATEGY	PAIR SPLITTING STRATEGY
YOUR HAND	YOUR HAND
2,2	**3,3**
DEALER SHOWS 3-7 2-7 if DASA B3	DEALER SHOWS 4-7 2-7 if DASA B4

PAIR SPLITTING STRATEGY	PAIR SPLITTING STRATEGY
YOUR HAND	YOUR HAND
4,4	**5,5**
NEVER 4-6 IF DASA B5	NEVER B6

PAIR SPLITTING STRATEGY	PAIR SPLITTING STRATEGY
YOUR HAND	**YOUR HAND**
6,6	**7,7**
DEALER SHOWS 2-6	DEALER SHOWS 2-7 2-8 IF DASA
B7	B8

PAIR SPLITTING STRATEGY	PAIR SPLITTING STRATEGY
YOUR HAND	**YOUR HAND**
8,8	**9,9**
ALWAYS	DEALER SHOWS 2-9 EXCEPT 7
B9	B10

PAIR SPLITTING STRATEGY	PAIR SPLITTING STRATEGY
YOUR HAND	**YOUR HAND**
10,10	**Ace, Ace**
NEVER	ALWAYS
B11	B12

SOFT DOUBLING STRATEGY

YOUR HAND

A,2
or **A,3**

DEALER
SHOWS
4-6   B13

SOFT DOUBLING STRATEGY

YOUR HAND

A,4
or **A,5**

DEALER
SHOWS
4-6   B14

SOFT DOUBLING STRATEGY

YOUR HAND

A,6

DEALER
SHOWS
2-6   B15

SOFT DOUBLING STRATEGY

YOUR HAND

A,7

DEALER
SHOWS
3-6   B16

SOFT DOUBLING STRATEGY

YOUR HAND

A,8

DEALER
SHOWS
6   B17

SOFT DOUBLING STRATEGY

YOUR HAND

A,9

NEVER   B18

HARD DOUBLING STRATEGY	HARD DOUBLING STRATEGY
YOUR HAND **5,3** **4,4**	YOUR HAND **9**
DEALER SHOWS 5 or 6 B19	DEALER SHOWS 2-6 B20
HARD DOUBLING STRATEGY	HARD DOUBLING STRATEGY
YOUR HAND **10**	YOUR HAND **11**
DEALER SHOWS 2-9 B21	ALWAYS B22
SOFT STANDING STRATEGY	SOFT STANDING STRATEGY
DEALER SHOWS **2-8**	DEALER SHOWS **9** or **10**
YOU STAND ON 18 B23	YOU STAND ON 19 B24

SOFT STANDING STRATEGY	HARD STANDING STRATEGY

SOFT STANDING STRATEGY

DEALER
SHOWS

ACE

YOU
STAND ON
18
19 IF
D STANDS
SOFT 17   B25

HARD STANDING STRATEGY

DEALER
SHOWS

2 or 3

YOU
STAND ON
13   B26

HARD STANDING STRATEGY

DEALER
SHOWS

4-6

YOU
STAND ON
12   B27

HARD STANDING STRATEGY

DEALER
SHOWS

7,8,9

or **A**

YOU
STAND ON
17   B28

HARD STANDING STRATEGY

DEALER
SHOWS

10

YOU
STAND ON
17 or
7,7   B29

HARD DOUBLING STRATEGY

YOUR
HAND

6-2

NEVER   B30

SURRENDER STRATEGY	SURRENDER STRATEGY
DEALER SHOWS	DEALER SHOWS
# ACE	# 10
SURRENDER (10,6) (9,7) D1	SURRENDER (10,6) (10,5) (9,7) (9,6) D2
PAIR SPLITTING STRATEGY	PAIR SPLITTING STRATEGY
YOUR HAND	YOUR HAND
2,2	**4,4**
DEALER SHOWS 4-7 2-7 IF DASA D3	NEVER 5 or 6 IF DASA D4
PAIR SPLITTING STRATEGY	PAIR SPLITTING STRATEGY
YOUR HAND	YOUR HAND
6,6	**7,7**
DEALER SHOWS 3-6 2-6 IF DASA D5	DEALER SHOWS 2-7 D6

SOFT DOUBLING STRATEGY	SOFT DOUBLING STRATEGY
YOUR HAND	YOUR HAND
A,2 **or A,3**	**A,6**
DEALER SHOWS 5 or 6 D7	DEALER SHOWS 3-6 D8
SOFT DOUBLING STRATEGY	HARD DOUBLING STRATEGY
YOUR HAND	YOUR HAND
A-8	**8**
NEVER D9	NEVER D10
HARD DOUBLING STRATEGY	HARD DOUBLING STRATEGY
YOUR HAND	YOUR HAND
9,2 **or 8,3**	**7,4** **or 6,5**
DEALER SHOWS 2-10 D11	ALWAYS D12

SOFT STANDING STRATEGY	HARD STANDING STRATEGY
DEALER SHOWS **ACE**	DEALER SHOWS **10**
YOU STAND ON 19 D13	YOU STAND ON 17 D14

SURRENDER STRATEGY	HARD DOUBLING STRATEGY
DEALER SHOWS **9**	YOUR HAND **9**
SURRENDER (10,6) (9,7) MB1	DEALER SHOWS 3-6 MB2

HARD DOUBLING STRATEGY

YOUR HAND **11**

DEALER SHOWS 2-10   MB3

SURRENDER STRATEGY

DEALER
SHOWS

ACE

SURRENDER
5-7 and
12-17   BAC1

SURRENDER STRATEGY

DEALER
SHOWS

10

SURRENDER
14-16   BAC2

BASIC STRATEGY FOR SINGLE DECK

SURRENDER STRATEGY

DEALER SHOWS	YOUR HAND
Ace	(10,6)
10	(10,6), (10,5)
	(9,7), (9,6),
	or (7,7)

PAIR SPLITTING STRATEGY

YOUR HAND	DEALER SHOWS
(2,2)	3–7 (*2–7)
(3,3)	4–7 (*2–7)
(4,4)	Never (*4–6)
(5,5)	Never
(6,6)	2–6
(7,7)	2–7 (*2–8)
(8,8)	Always
(9,9)	2–9 (Except 7)
(10,10)	Never
(Ace, Ace)	Always

DOUBLE AFTER SPLIT NOT ALLOWED
(*DOUBLE AFTER SPLIT ALLOWED)
DEALER STANDS ON SOFT 17
(**DEALER HITS SOFT 17)

BASIC STRATEGY FOR SINGLE DECK (con't)

SOFT DOUBLING STRATEGY

YOUR HAND	DEALER SHOWS
(Ace,2) or (Ace, 3)	4–6
(Ace,4) or (Ace,5)	4–6
(Ace,6)	2–6
(Ace,7)	3–6
(Ace,8)	6
(Ace,9)	Never

HARD DOUBLING STRATEGY

YOUR HAND	DEALER SHOWS
(5,3) or (4,4)	5 or 6
(6,2)	Never
9	2–6
10	2–9
11	Always

DOUBLE AFTER SPLIT NOT ALLOWED
(*DOUBLE AFTER SPLIT ALLOWED)
DEALER STANDS ON SOFT 17
(**DEALER HITS SOFT 17)

BASIC STRATEGY FOR SINGLE DECK (con't)

SOFT STANDING STRATEGY

DEALER SHOWS	YOU STAND ON
2–8	18
9 or 10	19
Ace	18 (**19)

HARD STANDING STRATEGY

DEALER SHOWS	YOU STAND ON
2 or 3	13
4–6	12
7,8 or Ace	17
9	17
10	17 or (7,7)

DOUBLE AFTER SPLIT NOT ALLOWED
(*DOUBLE AFTER SPLIT ALLOWED)
DEALER STANDS ON SOFT 17
(**DEALER HITS SOFT 17)

BASIC STRATEGY FOR SINGLE DECK
RENO-LAKE TAHOE RULES

PAIR SPLITTING STRATEGY

DEALER SHOWS	YOUR HAND
3–7	(2,2)
4–7	(3,3)
Never	(4,4)
Never	(5,5)
2–6	(6,6)
2–7	(7,7)
Always	(8,8)
2–9 (Except 7)	(9,9)
Never	(10,10)
Always	(Ace, Ace)

HARD DOUBLING STRATEGY

DEALER SHOWS	YOUR HAND
2–9	10
Always	11

DOUBLE AFTER SPLIT NOT ALLOWED
DEALER HITS SOFT 17

BASIC STRATEGY FOR SINGLE DECK
RENO-LAKE TAHOE RULES (con't)

SOFT STANDING STRATEGY

YOU STAND ON	DEALER SHOWS
18	2–8
19	9 or 10
19	Ace

HARD STANDING STRATEGY

YOU STAND ON	DEALER SHOWS
13	2 or 3
12	4–6
17	7,8, or Ace
17	9
17 or (7,7)	10

DOUBLE AFTER SPLIT NOT ALLOWED
DEALER HITS SOFT 17

BASIC STRATEGY FOR DOUBLE DECK

SURRENDER STRATEGY

DEALER SHOWS	YOUR HAND
Ace	(10,6) or (9,7)
10	(10,6), (10,5)
	(9,7) or (9,6)

PAIR SPLITTING STRATEGY

YOUR HAND	DEALER SHOWS
(2,2)	4-7 (*2-7)
(3,3)	4-7 (*2-7)
(4,4)	Never (*5 or 6)
(5,5)	Never
(6,6)	3-6, (*2-6)
(7,7)	2-7
(8,8)	Always
(9,9)	2-9 (Except 7)
(10,10)	Never
(Ace, Ace)	Always

DOUBLE AFTER SPLIT NOT ALLOWED
(*DOUBLE AFTER SPLIT ALLOWED)

BASIC STRATEGY FOR DOUBLE DECK (con't)

SOFT DOUBLING STRATEGY

YOUR HAND	DEALER SHOWS
(Ace, 2) or (Ace, 3)	5 or 6
(Ace, 4) or (Ace, 5)	4–6
(Ace, 6)	3–6
(Ace, 7)	3–6
(Ace, 8)	Never
(Ace, 9)	Never

HARD DOUBLING STRATEGY

YOUR HAND	DEALER SHOWS
8	Never
9	2–6
10	2–9
(9,2) or (8,3)	2–10
(7,4) or (6,5)	Always

DOUBLE AFTER SPLIT NOT ALLOWED
(*DOUBLE AFTER SPLIT ALLOWED)

BASIC STRATEGY FOR DOUBLE DECK (con't)

SOFT STANDING STRATEGY

DEALER SHOWS	YOU STAND ON
2–8	18
9 or 10	19
Ace	19

HARD STANDING STRATEGY

DEALER SHOWS	YOU STAND ON
2 or 3	13
4–6	12
7,8, or Ace	17
9	17
10	17

DOUBLE AFTER SPLIT NOT ALLOWED
(*DOUBLE AFTER SPLIT ALLOWED)

BASIC STRATEGY FOR FOUR OR MORE DECKS

SURRENDER STRATEGY

DEALER SHOWS	YOUR HAND
Ace	(10,6) or (9,7)
10	(10,6), (10,5)
	(9,7), or (9,6)
9	(10,6) or (9,7)

PAIR SPLITTING STRATEGY

YOUR HAND	DEALER SHOWS
(2,2)	4-7 (*2-7)
(3,3)	4-7 (*2-7)
(4,4)	Never (*5 or 6)
(5,5)	Never
(6,6)	3-6 (*2-6)
(7,7)	2-7
(8,8)	Always
(9,9)	2-9 (Except 7)
(10,10)	Never
(Ace, Ace)	Always

DOUBLE AFTER SPLIT NOT ALLOWED
(*DOUBLE AFTER SPLIT ALLOWED)

BASIC STRATEGY FOR FOUR
OR MORE DECKS (con't)

SOFT DOUBLING STRATEGY

YOUR HAND	DEALER SHOWS
(Ace, 2) or (Ace, 3)	5 or 6
(Ace, 4) or (Ace, 5)	4–6
(Ace, 6)	3–6
(Ace, 7)	3–6
(Ace, 8)	Never
(Ace, 9)	Never

HARD DOUBLING STRATEGY

YOUR HAND	DEALER SHOWS
8	Never
9	3–6
10	2–9
11	2–10

DOUBLE AFTER SPLIT NOT ALLOWED
(*DOUBLE AFTER SPLIT ALLOWED)

BASIC STRATEGY FOR FOUR
OR MORE DECKS (con't)

SOFT STANDING STRATEGY

DEALER SHOWS	YOU STAND ON
2–8	18
9 or 10	19
Ace	19

HARD STANDING STRATEGY

DEALER SHOWS	YOU STAND ON
2 or 3	13
4–6	12
7, 8, or Ace	17
9	17
10	17

DOUBLE AFTER SPLIT NOT ALLOWED
(*DOUBLE AFTER SPLIT ALLOWED)

BASIC STRATEGY FOR FOUR OR MORE DECKS (WITH *SINGLE DECK*[1] AND *DOUBLE DECK*[2] EXCEPTIONS, AS NOTED)

SURRENDER STRATEGY	
DEALER SHOWS	YOUR HAND
Ace	(10,6) or (9,7)
Ace[1]	(10,6) (Except 9,7)
10	(10,6), (10,5)
	(9,7), or (9,6)
10[1]	+(7,7)
9	(10,6) or (9,7)
9[1,2]	(Except 10,6 or 9,7)

PAIR SPLITTING STRATEGY	
YOUR HAND	DEALER SHOWS
(2,2)	4–7 (*2–7)
(2,2)[1]	3–7 (*2–7)
(3,3)	4–7 (*2–7)
(4,4)	Never (*5 or 6)
(4,4)[1]	Never (*4–6)
(5,5)	Never
(6,6)	3–6 (*2–6)
(6,6)[1]	2–6 (*2–7)
(7,7)	2–7
(7,7)[1]	2–7 (*2–8)
(8,8)	Always
(9,9)	2–9 (Except 7)
(10,10)	Never
(Ace, Ace)	Always

DOUBLE AFTER SPLIT NOT ALLOWED
(*DOUBLE AFTER SPLIT ALLOWED)
DEALER STANDS ON SOFT 17
(**DEALER HITS SOFT 17)

BASIC STRATEGY FOR FOUR OR MORE DECKS
(WITH *SINGLE DECK₁* AND *DOUBLE DECK₂*
EXCEPTIONS, AS NOTED) (con't)

SOFT DOUBLING STRATEGY

YOUR HAND	DEALER SHOWS
(Ace, 2) or (Ace, 3)	5 or 6
(Ace, 2)[1] or (Ace, 3)[1]	4–6
(Ace, 4) or (Ace, 5)	4–6
(Ace, 6)	3–6
(Ace, 6)[1]	2–6
(Ace, 7)	3–6
(Ace, 8)	Never
(Ace, 8)[1]	6
(Ace, 9)	Never

HARD DOUBLING STRATEGY

YOUR HAND	DEALER SHOWS
8	Never
(5,3)[1] or (4,4)[1]	5 or 6
(6,2)[1]	Never
9	3–6
9[1,2]	2–6
10	2–9
11	2–10
11[1,2]	Always
(9,2)[2] or (8,3)[2]	2–10
(7,4)[2] or (6,5)[2]	Always

DOUBLE AFTER SPLIT NOT ALLOWED
(*DOUBLE AFTER SPLIT ALLOWED)
DEALER STANDS ON SOFT 17
(**DEALER HITS SOFT 17)

BASIC STRATEGY FOR FOUR OR MORE DECKS
(WITH *SINGLE DECK*$_1$ AND *DOUBLE DECK*$_2$ EXCEPTIONS, AS NOTED) (con't)

SOFT STANDING STRATEGY

DEALER SHOWS	YOU STAND ON
2–8	18
9 or 10	19
Ace	19
Ace$_1$	18 (**19)

HARD STANDING STRATEGY

DEALER SHOWS	YOU STAND ON
2 or 3	13
4–6	12
7,8, or Ace	17
9	17
10	17
10$_1$	+(7,7)

DOUBLE AFTER SPLIT NOT ALLOWED
(*DOUBLE AFTER SPLIT ALLOWED)
DEALER STANDS ON SOFT 17
(**DEALER HITS SOFT 17)

BASIC STRATEGY FOR FOUR OR MORE DECKS ATLANTIC CITY RULES

SURRENDER STRATEGY*

DEALER SHOWS	YOUR HAND
Ace	5–7 and 12–17
10	14–16
9	(10,6) or (9,7)

PAIR SPLITTING STRATEGY

YOUR HAND	DEALER SHOWS
(2,2)	2–7
(3,3)	2–7
(4,4)	5 or 6
(5,5)	Never
(6,6)	2–6
(7,7)	2–7
(8,8)	Always
(9,9)	2–9, Except 7
(10,10)	Never
(Ace, Ace)	Always

In May, 1981, Atlantic City canceled the Surrender option. If Surrender is not reinstated, use Basic Strategy for Las Vegas 4 Decks, DASA, without Surrender.

BASIC STRATEGY FOR FOUR OR MORE DECKS
ATLANTIC CITY RULES (con't)

SOFT DOUBLING STRATEGY

YOUR HAND	DEALER SHOWS
(Ace, 2) or (Ace, 3)	5 or 6
(Ace, 4) or (Ace, 5)	4–6
(Ace, 6)	3–6
(Ace, 7)	3–6
(Ace, 8)	Never
(Ace, 9)	Never

HARD DOUBLING STRATEGY

YOUR HAND	DEALER SHOWS
8	Never
9	3–6
10	2–9
11	2–10

BASIC STRATEGY FOR FOUR OR MORE DECKS
ATLANTIC CITY RULES (con't)

SOFT STANDING STRATEGY

DEALER SHOWS	YOU STAND ON
2–8	18
9 or 10	19
Ace	19

HARD STANDING STRATEGY

DEALER SHOWS	YOU STAND ON
2 or 3	13
4–6	12
7,8 or Ace	17
9	17
10	17

KEEPING YOUR GAMING
KNOWLEDGE CURRENT

Now that you are well on your way to becoming a proficient Blackjack player, you will want to keep abreast of all the latest rule variations in the game in casinos around the world. *Gambling Times* magazine can give you that information.

Since February of 1977, readers of *Gambling Times* magazine have profited immensely. They have done so by using the information they have read each month. If that sounds like a simple solution to winning more and losing less, well it is! Readers look to *Gambling Times* for that very specific reason. And it delivers.

Gambling Times is totally dedicated to showing readers how to win more money in every form of legalized gambling. How much you're going to win depends on many factors, but it's going to be considerably more than the cost of a subscription.

WINNING AND MONEY

Winning, that's what *Gambling Times* is all about. And money, that's what *Gambling Times* is all about. Because winning and money go hand in hand.

Here's what the late Vince Lombardi, the famous football coach of the Green Bay Packers, had to say about winning:

"It's not a sometime thing. Winning is a habit. There is no room for second place. There is only one place in my game and that is first place. I have finished second twice in my time at Green Bay and I don't ever want to finish second again. The objective is to win—fairly, squarely, decently, by the rules—but to win. To beat the other guy. Maybe that sounds hard or cruel. I don't think it is. It is and has always been an American zeal to be first in anything we do, and to win, and to win and to win."

Mr. Lombardi firmly believed that being a winner is "man's finest hour." *Gambling Times* believes it is too, while being a loser is depressing, ego-deflating, expensive and usually very lonely. "Everybody loves a winner" may be a cliche, but it's true. Winners command respect and are greatly admired. Winners are also very popular and have an abundance of friends. You may have seen a winner in a casino, with a bevy of girls surrounding him. . .or remember one who could get just about any girl he wanted.

Some of the greatest gamblers in the world also have strong views on what winning is all about. Here's what two of them have to say on the subject:

"To be a winner, a man has to feel good about himself and know he has some kind of advantage going in. I never made bets on even chances. Smart is better than lucky."—"Titanic" Thompson

"When it comes to winnin', I got me a one-track mind. You gotta want to win more than anything else. And you gotta have confidence. You can't pretend to have it. That's no good. You gotta have it. You gotta know. Guessers are losers. Gamblin's just as simple as that."—Johnny Moss

Gambling Times will bring you the knowledge you need to come home a winner and come home in the money. For it is knowledge, the kind of knowledge you'll get in its pages, that separates winners from losers. It's winning and money that *Gambling Times* offers you. *Gambling Times* will be your working manual to winning wealth.

The current distribution of this magazine is limited to selected newsstands in selected cities. Additionally, at newsstands where it is available, it's being snapped up, as soon as it's displayed, by gamblers who know a sure bet when they see one.

So if you're serious about winning, you're best off subscribing to *Gambling Times*. Then you can always count on its being there, conveniently delivered to your mailbox—and what's more, it will be there one to two weeks before it appears on the newsstands. You'll be among the first to receive the current issue as soon as it comes off the presses, and being first is the way to be a winner.

Having every monthly issue of *Gambling Times* will enable you to build an "Encyclopedia of Gambling," since the contents of this magazine are full of sound advice that will be as good in five or ten years as it is now.

As you can see, a subscription to *Gambling Times* is your best bet for a future of knowledgeable gambling. It's your ticket to *WINNING* and *MONEY.*

Take the time to read the following offer. As you can see, *Gambling Times* has gone all out to give you outstanding bonuses. You can join the knowledgeable players who have learned that *Gambling Times* helps them to win more money.

FOUR NEW WAYS TO GET 12 WINNING ISSUES OF *GAMBLING TIMES* FREE...

Every month over 250,000 readers trust *Gambling Times* to introduce powerful new winning strategies and systems. Using proven scientific methods, the world's leading experts show you how to win big money in the complex field of gambling.

Gambling Times has shown how progressive slot machines can be beat. Readers have discovered important new edges in blackjack. They've been shown how to know for sure when an opponent is bluffing at poker. *Gambling Times* has also spelled out winning methods for football, baseball and basketball. They've published profound new ways of beating horses. Their team of experts will uncover information in the months ahead that's certain to be worth thousands of dollars to you.

In fact, the features are so revolutionary that they must take special precautions to make sure *Gambling Times* readers learn these secrets long before anyone else. So how much is *Gambling Times* worth to you? Well...

NOW *GAMBLING TIMES* CAN BE BETTER THAN FREE! Here's how: This BONUS package comes AUTOMATICALLY TO YOU WHEN YOU SUBSCRIBE...or goes to a friend if you give a gift subscription.

(1) POKER BONUS at the TROPICANA card room in Las Vegas. Play poker at the TROPICANA and receive a free dinner buffet and comps to the "Folies Bergere" show for you *and* a guest. Value exceeds $40 excluding gratuities.

(2) FREE SPORTS BET. CHURCHILL DOWNS SPORTS BOOK in Las Vegas will let you make one wager up to $300 with no "vigorish." This means instead of laying the usual 11-to-10 odds, you can actually bet even up! You can easily save $30 here.

(3) PAYOFF BIGGER THAN THE TRACK. LEROY'S RACE BOOK, in Las Vegas, will add 10% to your payoff (up to $30 extra) on a special bet. Just pick the horse and the race of your choice, anywhere in America. For the first time in history, you can win more than the track pays.

(4) OUTSTANDING ROOM DISCOUNTS available only to *Gambling Times* subscribers. Check in at the SANDS in Las Vegas or Atlantic City, the TROPICANA in Atlantic City, the HIGH SIERRA in Lake Tahoe, or the CONDADO INN & CASINO in San Juan, Puerto Rico. Stay for 3 days and 2 nights and you'll save $29 off their normal low rates.

THAT'S A SAVING GREATER THAN THE ENTIRE COST OF YOUR SUBSCRIPTION.

USE ALL FOUR CERTIFICATES (VALID FOR ONE YEAR)...GET *GAMBLING TIMES* FREE...AND YOU'LL PUT $93 IN YOUR POCKET!

To begin your delivery of *Gambling Times* magazine at once, enclose a payment of $36.00 by check or money order (U.S. currency), Master-Card or Visa. Add $5.00 per year for postage outside the United States.

Send payment to:

GAMBLING TIMES MAGAZINE
1018 N. Cole Avenue
Hollywood, California 90038

GAMBLING TIMES
MONEY BACK GUARANTEE

If at any time you decide *Gambling Times* is not for you, you will receive a full refund on all unmailed copies. You are under no obligation and may keep the bonus as a gift.

Other Valuable Sources of Knowledge
Available Through *Gambling Times*

Here are some additional sources you can turn to for worthwhile gambling information:

The Experts Sports Handicapping Newsletter.
Published monthly, this newsletter will show you how to become an Expert handicapper. You will learn the different styles of handicapping and be able to select the one method best suited to your personality. Yearly subscriptions are $60; $50 for *Gambling Times* subscribers.

The Experts Blackjack Newsletter.
This monthly newsletter has all the top blackjack Experts working just for you. Features answers, strategies and insights that were never before possible. Yearly subscriptions are $60; $50 for *Gambling Times* subscribers.

Poker Player.
Published every other week, this *Gambling Times* newspaper features the best writers and theorists on the poker scene today. You will learn all aspects of poker, from odds to psychology, as well as how to play in no-limit competition and in tournaments. Yearly subscriptions (26 issues) are $20.

Casino Marketing International.

CMI sponsors the largest prize-pool blackjack tournaments in the world. Using an exciting non-elimination format, CMI offers the tournament blackjack player the opportunity to play in each round of the tournament. In 1984 the Desert Inn in Las Vegas hosted the Blackjack Tournaments. In 1985 CMI expects to offer Blackjack Tournaments in Atlantic City and Reno/Lake Tahoe. For information on where and when the next tournaments will be held, write CMI, 8462 Sunset Boulevard, Penthouse Suite, Los Angeles, CA 90069, or call toll free (800) 421-4442. In California call (800) 252-7772.

Super/System: A Course in Power Poker by Doyle Brunson.

The bible for poker players. This book contains contributions from poker's leading professionals, including Bobby Baldwin, Mike Caro and David Sklansky. An encyclopedia of more than 600 pages of detailed strategy for every form of poker.

Hardbound. $50.00. (Total shipping charges: $2.50).

OTHER BOOKS AVAILABLE

If you can't find the following books at your local bookstore, they may be ordered directly from *Gambling Times,* 1018 N. Cole Ave., Hollywood, CA 90038. Information on how to order is on page *241*.

Blackjack Books

The Gambling Times Guide to Blackjack by Stanley Roberts with Edward O. Thorp, Ken Uston, Lance Humble, Arnold Snyder, Julian Braun, D. Howard Mitchell, Jerry Patterson, and other experts in this field—The top blackjack authorities have been brought together for the first time to bring to the reader the ins and outs of the game of blackjack. All aspects of the game are discussed. Winning techniques are presented for beginners and casual players.
Softbound. $5.95. (ISBN: 0-89746-015-4)

Million Dollar Blackjack by Ken Uston—Every blackjack enthusiast or gaming traveler who fancies himself a "21" player can improve his game with this explosive bestseller. Ken Uston shows you how he and his team won over 4 million dollars at blackjack. Now, for the first time, you can find out how he did it and how his system can help you. Includes playing and betting strategies, winning secrets, protection from cheaters, Uston's Advanced Point Count System, and a glossary of inside terms used by professionals.
Hardbound. $18.95. (ISBN: 0-914314-08-4)

Winning Blackjack by Stanley Roberts—It is the simplest, most accurate blackjack system ever devised. The average person takes about eight hours both to read the system completely and master it. It does not require a photographic memory. All you really have to do is pay attention to the game. Businessmen and housewives alike report consistent winnings of up to $500 a day when using this system. This manual is complete in every way. It not only tells you how to play, it also tells you where to play, how much to bet and some very important tips about the art of casino play. There is a special section for beating multi-deck games and everything you need to know about blackjack in Las Vegas, Reno, Tahoe,

Atlantic City and a host of other casino resorts around the world. This book has the power to completely transform your life! *Winning Blackjack* is large, 8½" × 11", and includes pull-apart flash cards printed on card stock.

Softbound. $95.00. (ISBN: 0-914314-00-9)

Poker Books

According to Doyle by Doyle Brunson—Acknowledged by most people as the world's best all-around poker player, twice World Champion Doyle Brunson brings you his homespun wisdom from over 30 years as a professional poker player. This book will not only show you how to win at poker, it will give you valuable insights into how to better handle that poker game called LIFE.
Softbound. $6.95. (ISBN: 0-89746-003-0)

Caro on Gambling by Mike Caro—The world's leading poker writer covers all the aspects of gambling from his regular columns in *Gambling Times* magazine and *Poker Player* newspaper. Discussing odds and probabilities, bluffing and raising, psychology and character, this book will bring to light valuable concepts that can be turned into instant profits in home games as well as in the poker palaces of the West.
Softbound. $6.95. (ISBN: 0-89746-029-4)

Caro's Book of Tells by Mike Caro—The photographic body language of poker. Approximately 150 photographs with text explaining when a player is bluffing, when he's got the winning hand—and WHY. Based on accurate investigation; it is NOT guesswork. Even the greatest of gamblers has some giveaway behavior. For the first time in print, one of the world's top poker players reveals how he virtually can read minds because nearly every player has a "tell." Seal the leaks in your poker game and empty your opponent's chip tray.
Hardbound. $20.00. (ISBN: 0-914314-04-1)

The Gambling Times Official Rules of Poker by Mike Caro—Settles home poker arguments. Caro has written the revised rule book (including a section on etiquette) for the Horseshoe Club in Gardena, California, that may soon be adopted by other clubs and become the California standard. He is presently scheduling a meeting of poker room managers

at the Palace Station in Las Vegas. This should lead to the creation of a uniform book of rules for Nevada cardrooms. *The Gambling Times Official Rules of Poker* includes sections of the rules from public cardrooms, but mostly it is for home poker. The book is needed because there presently exists no true authority for settling Friday night poker disputes.
Softbound. $5.95. (ISBN: 0-89746-012-X)

Poker for Women by Mike Caro—How women can take advantage of the special male-female ego wars at the poker table and win. This book also has non-poker everyday value for women. Men can be destroyed at the poker table by coy, cunning or aggressive women. That's because, on a subconscious level, men expect women to act traditionally. This book tells women when to flirt, when to be tough and when to whimper. Many of the tactics are tried and proven by Caro's own students. This book does not claim that women are better players, merely that there are strategies available to them that are not available to their male opponents.
Softbound. $5.95. (ISBN: 0-89746-009-X)

Poker Without Cards by Mike Caro—Applying world-class poker tactics to everyday life. Is the salesman bluffing? Can you get a better price? Negotiating is like playing a poker hand. Although poker tactics are common in daily encounters, few people realize when a hand is being played. It's hard to make the right decision when you're not even aware that you've been raised. The book is honest and accurate in its evaluation of behavior.
Softbound. $6.95. (ISBN: 0-89746-038-3)

Wins, Places, and Pros by Tex Sheahan—With more than 50 years of experience as a professional poker player and cardroom manager/tournament director, Tex lets his readers in on the secrets that separate the men from the boys at the poker table. Descriptions of poker events, playing experiences from all over the world, and those special personalities who are the masters of the game. . .Tex knows them all and lays it out in his marvelous easy-to-read style.
Softbound. $6.95. (ISBN: 0-89746-008-1)

Casino Games

The Gambling Times Guide to Casino Games by Len Miller—The co-founder and editor of *Gambling Times* magazine vividly describes the casino games and explains their rules and betting procedures. This easy-to-follow guide covers blackjack, craps, roulette, keno, video machines, progressive slots and more. After reading this book, you'll play like a pro!
Softbound. $5.95. (ISBN: 0-89746-017-0)

The Gambling Times Guide to Craps by N.B. Winkless, Jr.—The ultimate craps book for beginners and experts alike. It provides you with a program to tackle the house edge that can be used on a home computer. This text shows you which bets to avoid and tells you the difference between craps in Nevada and craps in other gaming resort areas. It includes a glossary of terms and a directory of dealer schools.
Softbound. $5.95. (ISBN: 0-89746-013-8)

General Interest Books

According to Gambling Times: The Rules of Gambling Games by Stanley Roberts—At last you can finally settle all the arguments regarding what the rules are in every known gambling endeavor. From pari-mutuels to bookie slips, from blackjack to gin rummy, the rules of the games and the variations that are generally accepted in both public and private situations are clearly enumerated by the world's #1 gaming authority.
Hardbound. $12.00. (ISBN: 0-914314-07-6)

The Gambling Times Guide to Gaming Around the World compiled by Arnold L. Abrams—The complete travel guide to legal gaming throughout the world. This comprehensive gaming guide lists casinos around the world; the games played in each; cardrooms and facilities; greyhound racing and horse racing tracks, as well as jai alai frontons, lotteries and sports betting facilities. This book is a must for the traveling gamer.
Softbound. $5.95. (ISBN: 0-89746-020-0)

The Gambling Times Guide to Systems That Win, Volume I and Volume II—For those who want to broaden their gambling knowledge, this two-volume set offers complete gambling systems used by the experts. Learn their strategies and how to incorporate them into your

gambling style. **Volume I** covers 12 systems that win for roulette, craps, backgammon, slot machines, horse racing, baseball, basketball and football.
Softbound. $5.95. (ISBN: 0-89746-034-0)
Volume II features 12 more systems that win, covering horse racing, craps, blackjack, slot machines, jai alai and baseball.
Softbound. $5.95. (ISBN: 0-89746-034-0)

The Gambling Times Guide to Winning Systems, Volume I and Volume II—For those who take their gambling seriously, *Gambling Times* presents a two-volume set of proven winning systems. Learn how the experts beat the house edge and become consistent winners. **Volume I** contains 12 complete strategies for casino games and sports wagering, including baccarat, blackjack, keno, basketball and harness handicapping.
Softbound. $5.95. (ISBN: 0-89746-032-4)
Volume II contains 12 more winning systems covering poker bluffing, pitching analysis, greyhound handicapping and roulette.
Softbound. $5.95. (ISBN: 0-89746-033-2)

Gambling Times Presents Winning Systems and Methods, Volume I and Volume II—This two-volume collection of winning strategies by some of the nation's leading experts on gambling will help you in your quest to beat the percentages. **Volume I** includes several chapters on blackjack, as well as methods for beating baseball, basketball, hockey, steeplechase and grass racing.
Softbound. $5.95. (ISBN: 0-89746-036-7)
Volume II contains an analysis of keno and video poker, as well as systems for success in sports betting and horse racing.
Softbound. $5.95. (ISBN: 0-89746-037-5)

The Mathematics of Gambling by Edward O. Thorp—The "Albert Einstein of gambling" presents his second book on the subject. His first book, *Beat The Dealer,* set the gambling world on its heels and struck fear into the cold-blooded hearts of Las Vegas casino-owners in 1962. Now, more than twenty years later, Dr. Thorp again challenges the odds by bringing out a simple to understand version of more than thirty years of exploration into all aspects of what separates winners from losers...knowing the real meaning of the parameters of the games.
Softbound. $7.95. (ISBN: 0-89746-019-7)

Odds: Quick and Simple by Mike Caro—How to know the right lines and win by figuring the odds logically. Common sense replaces mathematical formulas. This book will teach probabilities plainly and powerfully. The emphasis will be on gambling, showing how to quickly determine whether or not to make a wager. Particular emphasis will be on sports bets, pot odds in poker, dice and various proposition bets. Also included will be tables of the most important gambling odds (craps, roulette, poker, blackjack, keno) for easy reference.
Softbound. $5.95. (ISBN: 0-89746-030-8)

P$yching Out Vegas by Marvin Karlins, Ph.D.—The dream merchants who build and operate gaming resorts subtly work on the casino patron to direct his attention, control his actions and turn his pockets inside out. At last, their techniques are revealed to you by a noted psychologist who shows you how you can successfully control your behavior and turn a losing attitude into a lifetime winning streak.
Hardbound. $12.00. (ISBN: 0-914314-03-3)

Winning by Computer by Dr. Donald Sullivan—Now, for the first time, the wonders of computer technology are harnessed for the gambler. Dr. Sullivan explains how to figure the odds and identify key factors in all forms of race and sports handicapping.
Softbound. $5.95. (ISBN: 0-89746-018-9)

Sports Betting Books

The Gambling Times Guide to Basketball Handicapping by Barbara Nathan—This easy-to-read, highly informative book is the definitive guide to basketball betting. Expert sports handicapper Barbara Nathan provides handicapping knowledge, insightful coverage, and step-by-step guidance for money management. The advantages and disadvantages of relying on sports services are also covered.
Softbound. $5.95. (ISBN: 0-89746-023-5)

The Gambling Times Guide to Football Handicapping by Bob McCune— Starting with the novice's approach to handicapping football, and winding up with some of the more sophisticated team selection techniques in the sports handicapping realm, this book will actually tell the reader how to forecast, *in advance*, the final scores of most major national foot-

ball games. The author's background and expertise on the subject will put money into any sports gambler's pocket.
Softbound. $5.95. (ISBN: 0-89746-022-7)

The Gambling Times Guide to Greyhound Racing by William E. McBride—This complete discussion of greyhound racing is a must for anyone who is just beginning to appreciate this exciting and profitable sport. The book begins with a brief overview detailing the origins of greyhound racing and pari-mutuel betting, and explains the greyhound track environment, betting procedures, and handicapping methods. Includes an appendix of various greyhound organizations, a review of greyhound books, and an interesting section on famous dogs and personalities in the world of greyhound racing.
Softbound. $5.95. (ISBN: 0-89746-007-3)

The Gambling Times Guide to Harness Racing by Igor Kusyshyn, Ph.D., Al Stanley and Sam Dragich—Three of Canada's top harness handicapping authorities present their inside approach to analyzing the harness racing scene and selecting winners. All the important factors from the type of sulky, workouts, drivers' ratings, speed, pace, etc., are skillfully presented in simple terms that can be used by novices and experienced racegoers to find the likely winners.
Softbound. $5.95. (ISBN: 0-89746-002-2)

The Gambling Times Guide to Jai Alai by William R. Keevers—The most comprehensive book on jai alai available. Author Bill Keevers takes the reader on an informative journey from the ancient beginnings of the game to its current popularity. This easy-to-understand guide will show you the fine points of the game, how to improve your betting percentage, and where to find jai alai frontons.
Softbound. $5.95. (ISBN: 0-89746-010-3)

The Gambling Times Guide to Thoroughbred Racing by R.G. Denis—Newcomers to the racetrack and veterans alike will appreciate the informative description of the thoroughbred pari-mutuel activity supplied by this experienced racing authority. Activities at the track and available information are blended skillfully in this guide to selecting winners that pay off in big-ticket returns.
Softbound. $5.95. (ISBN: 0-89746-005-7)

UPCOMING *GAMBLING TIMES* BOOKS

The following books will be at your local bookstore by September, 1984. If you can't find them there, they may also be ordered directly from *Gambling Times*.

Poker Books

Caro's Poker Encyclopedia by Mike Caro—Features alphabetical definitions and discussions of poker terms. Extensively cross-indexed, it can be used as a reference book to look up important poker terms (ante, bluff, sandbag) or it can be pleasurably read straight through. The definitions are brief; the advice is in-depth.
Softbound. $8.95. (ISBN: 0-89746-039-1)

Free Money: How to Win in the Cardrooms of California by Michael Wiesenberg—Computer expert and poker writer par excellence, Michael Wiesenberg delivers critical knowledge to those who play in the poker rooms of the western states. Wiesenberg gives you the precise meaning of the rules as well as the mathematics of poker to aid public and private poker players alike. Wiesenberg, a prolific author, is published by more gaming periodicals than any other writer.
Softbound. $6.95. (ISBN: 0-89746-027-8)

The Railbird by Rex Jones—The ultimate kibitzer, the man who watches from the rail in the poker room, has unique insights into the character and performance of all poker players. From this vantage point, Rex Jones, Ph.D., blends his expertise and considerable education in anthropology with his lifetime of poker playing and watching. The result is a delightful book with exceptional values for those who want to avoid the fatal errors of bad players and capitalize upon the qualities that make up the winning strengths of outstanding poker players.
Softbound. $6.95. (ISBN: 0-89746-028-6)

Tales Out of Tulsa by Bobby Baldwin—Oklahoma-born Bobby Baldwin, the youngest player to ever win the World Championship of Poker, is considered to be among the top five poker players in the world. Known affectionately as "The Owl," this brilliant poker genius, wise beyond

his years, brings the benefits of his experience to the pages of this book. It's sure to stop the leaks in your poker game, and you will be amazingly ahead of your opponents in the very next game you play.
Softbound. $6.95. (ISBN: 0-89746-006-5)

World Class Poker, Play by Play by Mike Caro—Once again, Caro brings the world of poker to life. This time he gives us a one-card-at-a-time analysis of world class poker, with many card illustrations. This book includes discussions of professional tactics, then simulates game situations and asks the reader to make decisions. Next, Caro provides the answer and the hand continues. This learn-while-you-pretend-to-play format is a favorite teaching method of Caro's and one which meets with a great deal of success.
Hardbound. $20.00. (ISBN: 0-914314-06-08)

General Interest Books

Caro on Computer Gambling by Mike Caro—Caro discusses computers and how they will change gambling. He provides winning systems and descriptions of actual programs. This book will give the novice a taste of how computers work. Using the Pascal programming language, Caro builds a working program step-by-step to show how a computer thinks and, also, how a human should analyze gambling propositions. This book is only slightly technical and mostly logical. Also discussed are ways that computers can cheat and speculation on the future of computers in gambling. Will you be able to type in your horse bets from your home computer? Can that personal computer be linked by phone into a perpetual poker game with the pots going straight into your bank account? The answers to these questions are found right here in Caro's book.
Softbound. $6.95. (ISBN: 0-89746-042-1)

The Gambling Times Quiz Book by Mike Caro—Learn while testing your knowledge. Caro's book includes questions and answers on the concepts and information published in previous issues of *Gambling Times*. Caro tells why an answer is correct and credit is given to the author whose *Gambling Times* article suggested the question. This book covers only established fact, not the personal opinions of authors, and Caro's inimitable style makes this an easy-reading, easy-learning book
Softbound. $5.95. (ISBN: 0-89746-031-6)

How the Superstars Gamble by Ron Delpit—Follow the stars to the racetracks, ball games, casinos and private clubs. You'll be amazed at how involved these world famous personalities are in the gambling scene, and how clever they are at the games they play. Ron Delpit, lifelong horse racing fan and confidant of innumerable showbiz greats, tells you fascinating tales about his friends, the superstars, with startling heretofore secret facts.
Hardbound. $12.00. (ISBN: 0-914314-17-3)

How to Win at Gaming Tournaments by Haven Earle Haley—Win your share of the millions of dollars and fabulous prizes being awarded to gaming contestants, and have the glory of being a World Champion. Poker, gin rummy, backgammon, craps, blackjack and baccarat are all popular tournament games. The rules, special tournament regulations, playing procedures, and how to obtain free entry are fully explained in this informative manual. The tournament promoters—who they are, where they hold events—and the cash and prizes awarded are explained in detail. Tournament play usually requires special strategy changes, which are detailed in this book.
Softbound. $8.95. (ISBN: 0-89746-016-2)

You're Comped: How to Be a Casino Guest by Len Miller—If you're a player you don't have to pay! Learn how to be "comped" in luxury casino-resort hotels the world over. A list of casinos together with names and addresses of junket representatives are included in this revealing guidebook. How to handle yourself on a junket is important if you want to receive all that you've been promised and be invited back again. How to do this, along with what you can expect from the casino, is explained in detail.
Softbound. $7.95. (ISBN: 0-89746-041-3)

Sports Betting Books

Fast Track to Harness Racing Profits by Mark Cramer——This systematic analysis of nuances in past performances will uncover patterns of improvement which will lead to flat bet profits. This book provides a functioning balance between creative handicapping and mechanical application.
Softbound. $6.95. (ISBN: 0-89746-026-X)

Fast Track to Thoroughbred Profits by Mark Cramer—A unique approach to selecting winners, with price in mind, by distinguishing between valuable and common-place information. Results: higher average pay-offs and solid flat bet profits. How to spot signs of improvement and when to cash in. And much, much more.
Softbound. $6.95. (ISBN: 0-89746-025-1)

Ordering Information

Send your book order along with your check or money order to:

Gambling Times
1018 N. Cole Ave.
Hollywood, CA 90038

Softbound Books: Please add $1.00 per book if delivered in the United States, $1.50 in Canada or Mexico, and $3.50 for foreign countries.

Hardbound Books: Shipping charges for the following books are $2.50 if delivered in the United States, $3.00 in Canada or Mexico, and $5.00 for foreign countries:
According to Gambling Times: The Rules of Gambling Games
Caro's Book of Tells
How the Superstars Gamble
Million Dollar Blackjack
P$yching Out Vegas
World Class Poker, Play by Play